YOUR GOLDEN SHADOW

Why Do Christians Break Down?
Big Kids' Mother Goose
When Going to Pieces Holds You Together
You Count, You Really Do
Conversations
Make Friends with Your Shadow
Prayers at Midpoint
The Joy of Feeling Good

YOUR GOLDEN SHADOW
Discovering and Fulfilling
Your Undeveloped Self

William A. Miller

1817

Harper & Row, Publishers, San Francisco

New York, Grand Rapids, Philadelphia, St. Louis
London, Singapore, Sydney, Tokyo, Toronto

Sources of Scripture quotations are noted (NIV, RSV, JB). When not noted, the translation is the author's own paraphrase; p. 22, p. 31, p. 79.

FIRST EDITION

Library of Congress Cataloging-in-Publication Data

Miller, William A., 1931–
  Your golden shadow: discovering and fulfilling your undeveloped
self / William A. Miller.—1st. ed.
    p. cm.
  ISBN 0-06-065717-0
  1. Self-realization.   2. Shadow (Psychoanalysis)   I. Title.
BF637.S4M55   1989
158'.1—dc20
                                                                89-45184
                                                                    CIP

---

89 90 91 92 93   RRD   10 9 8 7 6 5 4 3 2 1

to
my family:
Marilyn
Mark, Dana, and Taylor
Eric
Mom

Contents

Introduction   ix

PART ONE   The Journey

1 The Story of Shadow   3
2 The Journey Inward   17
3 The Benefits of Knowing Yourself   27
4 Overcoming the Interference of the Outer World   37
5 Pathways into the Shadow   51

PART TWO   The Discovery

6 Gold in the Mire   65
7 Scoundrels and Saints   77
8 The Undeveloped Self   87

PART THREE   The Fulfillment

9   The Power of Self-image   103
10 The Willingness to Risk   113
11 The Value of Failure   125
12 The Excitement of Creating   133
13 Resolution and Determination   141

Notes   147
About the Author   149

Introduction

This is a book about discovery: about discovering good things about yourself; about discovering positive and exciting aspects of yourself that you weren't sure were there; about discovering your potential for a richer experience of life and a greater sense of fulfillment.

A veritable gold mine of possibilities is hidden within each of us—aptitudes, attitudes, characteristics, and traits that once may have been conscious, but for some reason slipped away or were pushed away into our unconscious. In addition, there is great potential within each of us that has never had the opportunity to see the light of day.

We can be much more than we are. Researchers regularly remind us that we utilize only a small portion of our potential for development. No matter how long we live, most of us tap into only a comparatively tiny portion of the vast internal resources available to us.

The great reservoir of possibilities is our hidden self, or *shadow*. Our shadow is our "private life," as compared to the "public life" of our personality. This private life is *so* private that is is largely unknown even to ourselves. Our shadow is an unconscious force within us—a source of power and possibility that we can bring into consciousness and use creatively and constructively for a fuller and more enriching experience of life.

Because all human beings are capable of both great good and great evil, our shadow is likewise a source of both. The usual treatment of shadow is to perceive it as a dark, sinister counterpart to the bright *persona* we present to the world. Our shadow certainly is all that—it possesses the potential for the enactment of great evil. But the shadow is much more than that. It is the potential resource for the enactment of great good. It can be the gold mine of our lives, and we may enter it to uncover its treasures and bring them to the surface.

Most of us intuitively know that there *is* more to us than meets the eye, but we are uncertain about how to bring the gold of shadow into consciousness. We may also be reluctant to act on a revelation of our Golden Shadow when, of its own accord, it taps us on the shoulder and suggests, "Try this."

In this book I hope to provide the necessary help and direction to enable us to move into the recesses of our shadow and utilize creatively its positive possibilities for our lives. The book provides pathways by which we may enter our shadow, and resources for surmounting the obstacles that may hinder progress along our journey. We find many ways to bring the shadow's gold to the surface—to consciousness—and use it advantageously. We meet people not unlike ourselves, who have made their journey inward, struggled along its path, and emerged with treasures that enabled them to become much more of what they could be.

Many people in their later years say, "If I could live my life again, I would take more risks, be more assertive, and exercise greater self-discipline." The discovery and fulfillment of our undeveloped selves speaks directly to these concerns. We don't have to wish for another chance at life: All of us, if we wish, can make these changes now.

This book is divided into three parts, which together comprise the essence of the experience: the journey, the discovery, and the fulfillment. In part 1 we define the great journey inward that will bring us to our shadow's gold. In part 2 we discover the specifics of our own unique treasure. In part 3 we explore the hurdles we must pass and the resources available to us.

I have generally used the editorial form "we" as subject, rather than "you," "they," or "one." As author, I am as much involved in the process of discovering and fulfilling the Golden Shadow as are you who read these pages. I feel more comfortable perceiving this endeavor as a collective enterprise.

The concept for this book arose from a discussion with my friend and colleague, Jerry Davis, Clinical Pastoral Director at Loma Linda University Medical Center in Loma Linda, California. Following a seminar on "The Shadow" that I had presented at the medical center in the summer of 1987, Jerry encouraged me to elaborate more on the positive potential resident within this dark and hidden brother/sister. After that discussion I promised I would, and this is the result: *Your Golden Shadow.*

Part I

THE JOURNEY

CHAPTER 1

The Story of Shadow

A concept such as the "the Golden Shadow" conjures up all sorts of images in our minds. Shadows themselves are not particularly inviting; they seem to bode ill because of their darkness. We are almost intuitively reluctant to approach darkness because of the unknown and the indistinguishable within it.

Gold, on the other hand, is highly to be desired. It is precious and valuable; it offers promise because of its great potential. We are drawn to it and eagerly surrender to its drawing power, hoping to possess it and capitalize on the multitude of possibilities it promises.

How can there be gold in the shadow? The concept of "Golden Shadow" almost appears to be a contradiction . . . unless, of course, it is possible to perceive the brilliance of gold in the darkness of shadows. The concept becomes intriguing as we consider the possibility, and our interest grows cautiously. We want to seek the gold, and this desire gives us more courage to risk the foreboding darkness and the unknown of shadows. Soon we are on our journey, our quest for the Golden Shadow.

This is an internal quest, so we must outfit ourselves accordingly. We will need a map of the psyche, that marvelous dynamic entity that connects for us the inner and outer worlds, our two great realms of experience and sources of learning. Standing in the psyche somewhere between these two realms is *ego* or self—the "I" of whom I am aware in my waking life. When I look forward to the outer world I perceive, standing between ego and outer world, my *persona*—that image or "mask" through which I relate to my outer world. When I look backward to the inner world, I perceive something standing between ego and inner world. It is my *shadow*—that dimension in psyche through which I relate to my inner world. Viewing shadow is the most awesome part of the orientation; but even here, as we continue to look at its lack of light and corresponding undesirability, we may already gain a glimpse of some positive values hidden in shadow's darkness. So with this, the journey into the Golden Shadow has begun.

THE STORY OF TIM

Tim's growing-up experience was relatively uneventful, except for the fact that his father was hard to please. He had a way for doing everything, and his way was the only right way. He wasn't overtly abusive, but he let Tim know every time he wasn't doing something right—that is, every time Tim wasn't doing it his father's way.

Tim remembers many of the times his father gently criticized him for "doing it wrong." "He even told me more than once that I was turning the channel selector on the television set the wrong way to get from one channel to another. I just always turned it the way that was the shortest route," he said. "But my father said that was wrong. You should always go upward in the sequence of numbers when you turn the dial. It didn't seem to make any difference, but it surely did to him."

Tim's family was strongly religious, and that influence encouraged him to pursue a vocation that would help people. Tim had been fascinated by computers even when he was a small boy, but there was no encouragement for Tim to pursue anything in that field. Instead, he trained to become a social worker.

After college Tim took a job with a social service department, and a few months later he married Mary, the woman he had dated for eight years. Tim recalls that the night before their wedding day, his father asked him, "Are you sure this is what you want to do?" "I couldn't believe he said that," said Tim. "I mean, we had gone together for *eight years,* and he asked me if I was sure I really wanted to marry her. He never gave me credit for having any smarts at all."

Tim's performance as a social worker was acceptable, but nothing more; it was mediocre and perfunctory at best, and he found no real satisfaction or fulfillment in his work. In time, he began to be cynical and resentful toward many of the clients in his case load. He manifested none of this in his behavior, however; he was always the smiling, pleasing Tim.

One night he dreamed that a sinister intruder had broken into his house. In the dream Tim saw this underworld-type man go into the kitchen and ransack the room, smashing dishes, throwing pots and pans against the wall, and pulling down shelves from the cabinets, while Tim quietly looked on. He awoke frightened and bewildered by the dream.

Shortly after this experience he had a major quarrel with his supervisor, who had confronted him with his now less-than-acceptable performance. Tim's cynicism finally broke through in the quarrel. "It's a foolish waste to work with these people," he shouted. "They don't want to change; they don't want to do anything they don't have to do."

Some weeks later, after another similar episode with his supervisor, Tim abruptly quit his job. Fortunately Mary had part-time employment, which provided enough income to pay the bills while Tim was unemployed. His impulsive behavior, however, created considerable stress in the marriage.

I first met Tim about two months after he left his job. He was quite despondent, very critical of himself, and frightened about the uncertainty of his future. We began by talking together about his poor self-image, his relationship with his father, and what had happened at the department. "I'm a beat-up person," he said. "I live in a beat-up house and I drive a beat-up car. I don't want to do the only thing I'm trained to do, and I don't have the smarts to do anything else."

As time went on and we talked together, Tim journeyed inward, into his hidden shadow self. His discoveries were both frightening and uplifting. He encountered a sad man who wished for, even longed for his father's love and acceptance. He encountered a very angry man who wanted to wreck and smash things to vent the feelings he had held inside for years. He discovered an aggressive man who, in one of his fantasies, wanted to throw a jar of mayonnaise against the wall to see it smash and shatter and smear. He also encountered a strong and loving man—something of the opposite of the "beat-up" person he perceived himself to be.

Tim was able to recognize the strongly aggressive element in his shadow, which was probably the underworld figure who broke up the kitchen in his dream. Though frightening, this dimension promised the possibility that Tim could consciously use its positive aspect of assertiveness in a constructive and helpful way. His self-image improved and his self-esteem grew as he began to be able to accept his father as he was, even in his error of putting Tim down. He wept bitter tears as he let go of his need to change his father. "He will probably never be any different; but I don't have to go on believing he is right and trying to please him." Gradually, Tim brought forward his strong and accepting hidden self and began to develop, perhaps for the first time, a genuine self-respect.

One night he dreamed he was fishing. He had been fishing for a long time and hadn't even had so much as a nibble. He reeled in his line and discovered that his bait was a tiny horse—a tiny *dead* horse. "I was amazed by the imagery of this dream," he said. "At first it didn't make sense; except that I probably would never catch any fish that way. But then I remembered that Bible story where Jesus enlisted some of his disciples who were fishermen, and he told them he would make them fishers of men. I think I still want to do something that will help people—not necessarily in a religious sense—but it's not social work. That's the dead horse. Trying to help people by being a social worker is *for me* like fishing with a dead horse. It's got to be something else."

The "something else" for Tim turned out to be computer programming. One day as he practiced his meditation he visualized his boyhood and saw himself sitting at a keyboard excitedly operating a computer. His initial response to this possibility was, "Yeah, I could help people by doing that, except I could never do it; I just don't have the smarts." In time he discovered that he *could* do it; in fact, he graduated from the training program with the highest marks in his class. He is employed today as a programmer in a large financial corporation.

Tim's journey into his shadow was arduous and lengthy, but his discoveries of gold in that shadow turned his life around into an experience of satisfaction and greater fulfillment of his potential. Because of that journey inward, Tim is becoming much more of what he can be.

AN OVERVIEW OF OUR DEVELOPMENT

Tim is a person very much like you and me. Of course, no two lives are the same; but at least in broad brush strokes, our development as human beings is rather similar. It may be helpful to envision the process of our development as though we were shopkeepers assigned to selling ourselves to a highly selective and discriminating public: In the process of growing up we continually place various aspects of our potential personality on the trading counter with the hope that the public will buy them. When a certain trait or characteristic fits the expectations of the public (that is, family members, people we know in our community, and society in general) it becomes a part of our developing personality because it is acceptable. It "sells."

When we place a potential trait or characteristic out on that trading counter and it is not acceptable to the public, we are told so in clear terms: "That is not appropriate. Get that out of here and don't let us see it again." We quickly remove this trait or characteristic from the trading counter and stash it out of sight so that no one ever sees it again.

Not infrequently, a potential trait of characteristic, attitude, or aptitude is neither accepted nor rejected by the public. No one offers a favorable word; no one offers a discouraging word. No one offers any word at all. It just sits on the trading counter and collects dust.

We like it, though—this element that does nothing to stir the public either way—and we may even embrace it briefly. It could be scientific curiosity, or playing the guitar, or becoming an architect, or being assertive, or a passion for poetry or internal combustion engines. But in time we remove it from the trading counter and occupy ourselves with traits, characteristics, expressed feelings, talents, abilities, and interests that are proven sellers. This poor element that aroused no response gets put back on the shelf and is promptly forgotten, even though we may fully intend at some later time to test it again for acceptability and support.

Thus, to a very significant degree, personality develops through the process of trial and error. If it is true that we are created with the potential for virtually all possible traits, characteristics, attitudes, and abilities (be they positive or negative), it is likewise true that out of that vast array, we choose those elements that will get our needs met and our wants fulfilled as we develop our personalities. It is largely the immediate environment that determines what gets developed into conscious personality and what gets rejected into our shadow.

AN INTRODUCTION TO OPPOSITES: PERSONA AND SHADOW

The first verse of the Bible tells us, "In the beginning, God created the heavens and the earth" (Gen. 1:1 NIV); and that proclamation plunges us immediately into an awareness of the existence of opposites. Quickly following this announcement, the writer of the book of Genesis tells us that God created light and separated it from darkness, thus identifying another set of opposites. In a few more verses, the writer then speaks of the separation of the land from the waters. Thus, within the first ten verses of the first book of the Bible, the concept of opposites is firmly established and its significance and importance powerfully stated.

In world mythology, the creation and formation of the world almost universally involves a division into opposites. Out of the polarity of these opposites arises the power that molds the cosmos. For example, in Chinese mythology the cosmic symbol of the interchangeable polarity of opposites is the *yin-yang* figure. Yin, representing the earth element, is black, dark, and moist. Yang, representing heaven, is white, firm, and bright. The germ of each is present in the other, and each contains its opposite.

A fascinating Egyptian creation myth tells of Atum, the first deity, who stood alone as the primal being of all. One day he spat forth twin children from his mouth and named them Shu and Tefnut. Shu and Tefnut in time came together and produced from their union a second pair of twins whose names were Nut and Geb. Geb became the earth and appeared as a giant at rest, stretched out, lying on his back. His sister, Nut, made herself manifest in the Milky Way, bending down and arching herself like a bridge over Geb's body.

This love of Earth and Sky brought forth other pairs of twins— Osiris and Isis, and Set and Nephthys. Osiris and Isis appeared as deities who were intensely sympathetic to the human condition; they were sorrowing, sensitive, suffering beings. Set and Nephthys, on the other hand, lived out the power of dark, destructive forces. Egyptian mythology identified the presence of these opposites as significant and necessary, for without the "cleansing" presence of Set and Nephthys, life would be an unbalanced experience of only light, goodness, and superabundance.

The presence of opposites is as universal in reality as it is in myth and fantasy. As human beings, this presence is within us, too, "in the beginning." Each of us comes onto the scene of life as a being capable of great good, and great evil. As we mature, we too know within ourselves the qualities of light and darkness. The existence of opposites continues and increases and becomes firmly entrenched as an integral part of our being.

In the process of developing our conscious personalities, each of us endeavors to build an appearance that will be acceptable to and approved by the culture and subculture in which we live. For most of us this will mean the development of a personality, or persona, that will essentially conform to the moral values and laws virtually universally accepted and embodied in such codes of living as the Ten Commandments. It will also mean adherence to the specific system of values and expectations imposed by the subculture within which we develop. This is extremely important to every developing human being; for even as tiny infants we realize in a rudimentary way that we will have to abide by these mandates and fulfill these expectations if we are to be accepted by our culture and subculture, and in that acceptance have our needs met and our wants fulfilled.

Our personal subculture is the milieu in which we develop. It is essentially comprised of parents, extended family, religious teachings held by the family, racial and nationalistic values and expectations; and, as we mature, we add our peer group and other adults close to us. The mandates and expectations of our subculture are very simple to begin with, but become increasingly complex as we mature.

As our personality emerges out of our unconscious, we adopt and embody those traits, characteristics, attitudes, and aptitudes that will allow us to be accepted within our subculture. We undoubtedly have an innate predisposition to develop certain traits and characteristics; but the greatest portion are chosen in order to develop a personality that will please the subculture and which the subculture will in turn accept, reward, and identify as "ideal."

We reject and repress into our unconscious *shadow* traits, characteristics, attitudes, and aptitudes that are inconsistent with and unacceptable to our subculture. This is an unconscious and automatic process early in life; but as self-consciousness blooms within us, our choices become more conscious and deliberate.

Subcultures and subsocieties influence the development of every person, above and beyond the values of society in general. We need, therefore, to avoid generalizations, and speak in terms of subcultures that are unique to the developing personality. For values do vary, and what is acceptable and indeed desirable in one subculture (your public high school, for example) may be quite unacceptable and undesirable in another (the small, private college in which you are now enrolled). The general dimensions of the desirable (ideal) personality may be universal; but the more detailed aspects must be considered strictly on the basis of the expectations of the subculture in which a personality develops.

THE LAW OF OPPOSITES

Since the development of a conscious personality means that we must identify with something, and thus automatically reject its opposite, a certain law of opposites will prevail. This means that for every trait, characteristic, attitude, and aptitude that we draw up into the persona, its opposite—equal in magnitude—we reject and relegate to the shadow side.

For example, the child who has realized that an attitude of submissiveness will get her needs met and wants fulfilled (1) will help ensure acceptance in the subculture, and will be rewarded in some fashion or other; (2) will be highly motivated to incorporate that characteristic in her persona; and (3) will unconsciously posit the opposite attribute of rebelliousness in her shadow. Likewise the child who tests out an expression of angry disobedience to a parent and is severely punished for it will probably deny further expressions of such feelings and relegate them to the shadow, while simultaneously developing a persona of cheerful obedience. This is particularly true if the child tests out such a form of behavior more than once and is punished even more severely the second time.

Suppose Jimmy becomes upset with daddy because, either rightly or wrongly, daddy will not allow Jimmy to have his way. In anger Jimmy cries and shouts, "You're a mean daddy, and I don't like you any more!" Suppose also that daddy slaps Jimmy across the face so powerfully that his mouth becomes bloodied, then grabs the sobbing child and menacingly says, "Don't you *dare* talk to me like that ever again!"

Or suppose Lucy becomes upset with daddy because, either rightly or wrongly, daddy will not allow her to have her way. In anger Lucy cries and shouts, "You're a mean daddy, and I don't like you any more!" Suppose also that daddy quietly but sternly says to Lucy, "You shouldn't be angry. Being angry is not good. God does not like anger. God wants people to be nice. God will not love you if you are angry."

Whether the abusive response to the child is overt, as in the first illustration, or covert, as in the second, the result will be the same. The characteristics of being obedient, submissive, and pleasant will become firmly fixed in the persona of the developing child, while the opposite dimensions of disobedience, rebellion, and anger will constellate in the shadow. Furthermore, the magnitude and intensity of this negative material in the shadow will equal the magnitude and intensity of the "desirable" traits in the persona.

In this milieu, the expression of rebellion and anger, whether appropriate or not, is totally unacceptable. It is punished either by a blow to the face and a destructive threat; or, in a more "humane" manner, by the threat of the withdrawal of God's love. In either case, the child will either consciously or unconsciously conclude: "This attitude and characteristic does not get my needs met and my wants fulfilled. It does not allow me to be accepted in this subculture and milieu; therefore I must reject it, relegate it to the shadow world (ostensibly never to be seen or heard again), and replace it with its opposite."

The intensity and magnitude of traits, characteristics, and attributes of the persona are equalled by their counterparts in the shadow. Thus people who (by virtue of the expectations of the surrounding subculture) develop a strong attitude and demeanor of peacefulness, possess likewise in their shadow an equally powerful potential for warring.

A woman once asked me, "Do you mean to say that the more I love my husband, the more I have within me the potential to destroy him?" The answer, of course, is, "Yes, precisely." Many people hearing this are quite shocked and refuse to believe it. Many fail to hear the word "potential," and that is crucial to the statement. But even if they do hear it they simply do not want to believe that they are capable of murder. What is distressing is the fact that those who most strongly deny their shadow potential are the very ones most likely to be overcome by it.

We are all shocked every time we read or hear of another instance of ax slayings or shotgun murders where a person has killed several family members or colleagues, or has shot down passersby from a sniper's perch in a tower or tree. Often it is the act of a young person whose entire immediate family is destroyed in the rampage.

Such a murderer is often identified as a "good" person—kind, generous, law-abiding, charitable, religious; in short, "the last person one would expect to do such a thing." People who knew the murderer closely are heard to make statements such as, "I can't believe it; I won't believe it"; and, "He was such a shining example, it simply cannot be."

PARENTAL INFLUENCE

In the experience of the developing personality parents (biological or surrogate) are usually the most powerful influence. This is true because parents usually have the greatest and most enduring contact with the child. Therefore much of the child's personality is shaped by the expectations of the parents, wittingly or unwittingly. One may argue about the influence of heredity versus environment, and that argument will probably go on forever. It would be foolish to claim that environment (the subculture and milieu) alone shaped the personality, and heredity might have only to do with physical characteristics. It would be equally foolish to claim the opposite, that genetics is everything and environment is nothing.

We do know for a fact that the influence of adults (teachers, religious figures, and particularly mother and father) on the developing personality is powerful, and that babies and young children are constantly receiving and processing messages of all kinds and in all forms (voice, touch, glance) given to them by these impressive figures. Much of the child's personality will crystalize as a result of the child's response to the perceived expectations of the immediate environment embodied in these adults.

Parents sometimes wonder why their various children have such differing personalities. They forget that they themselves were different people in the rearing process of each child, even if the physical environment was stable and constant. This is true even in the case of identical twins. Twins may be physically identical, but be strikingly different in personality. Parents may be at the same point in time in the process of rearing twins, but this does not mean that their relationship to each child is identical. It is much too easy to overlook unconscious factors that may be powerfully sensed by children, but totally unknown to parents.

A man once told me, "I had no reason to doubt that my parents were sincere when they said they loved all us kids equally and had no favorites. They truly believed that. But I could read the difference in mom's eyes when she looked at the paper I brought home from school, and when she looked at my brother John's. She would commend us both and say how happy and proud she was. But it was there—in her face, in her eyes, in her quick glance—she liked my paper; but she was delighted with his."

Parents ought not to be discouraged by the realization that they do not always give the message they consciously intend to give. This observation is simply one of many reasons for "knowing ourselves" and being as conscious and aware of our own shadow elements as we can. We can never expect ourselves as parents to be totally free of the flaws of our human nature; but being more aware of that part of us about which we instinctively care to know very little—our own shadow—will enable us to be less controlled by its vagaries.

THE INFLUENCE OF CLOSED AND OPEN SUBCULTURES

The more monolithic, rigid, demanding, authoritarian, narrow, and legalistic the immediate environment in which one develops, the thicker is the persona and the more massive is the shadow. Conversely, the more supportive, confrontive, accepting, open, experimental, and caring the immediate subculture or milieu, the less thick the persona and the less massive the shadow.

In the restrictive experience, much of what is natural to humanity and the individual development of the human being must be denied because it simply cannot or will not be tolerated—it presents too great a threat to that milieu. Jimmy's authoritarian father, for example, is a very insecure person with low self-esteem. Anger addressed at him is so threatening that it can have no place and must therefore be denied and repressed. Any parent knows that anger is a valid human emotion and feeling and that children *do* become angry. In this instance, however, the child must reject anger rather than accept it and express it appropriately. To be accepted in that milieu the child must present a "face" of submission, pleasantness, and obedience. The face is a false face, masking true feelings. As time goes on and the experience is repeated—that is, if the child continues to mask anger with pleasantness—the mask will become thicker with each additional layer (episode) and the shadow more massive. In time the process of falsifying feelings will become "second nature," as we say, and will be totally unconscious.

The expression of anger is, of course, only one example. The child who develops in such a milieu may find it expedient to repress tears (sadness, grief, hurt), disappointment, exuberant joy, and a whole host of emotions and feelings natural to the human being. Natural sexual curiosity may have to be repressed by the child because the child is told, "That is dirty and nice people do not talk about such things." Natural ambition may have to be repressed because, "We learn to be content, whatever our lot." And on and on, so that the developing personality becomes an extremely thick persona sitting on a shadow full of dynamite. A thick persona means inauthenticity and artificiality. A massive shadow means being severely out of touch with oneself and vulnerable to the powers of one's negative unconscious.

In the expansive milieu, the developing personality creates a far thinner persona and a far less massive shadow. In this open, caring, confrontive, and supportive atmosphere, that which is recognized as part of being human is accepted. The developing child learns to feel free in expressing himself or herself within the bounds of propriety, without having to bear painful consequences. There is little need to "pretend" to be substantially other than one is, and to bury one's authentic self.

Despite our many efforts, however, the persona is never absolutely in accord with what is expected of us in our immediate subculture or in the larger culture of which we are a part. The "ideal" personality remains just that—ideal. Even if the motivator for developing personality is the desire and need to be accepted (and correspondingly get our needs met and wants fulfilled) it is never enough to drive us to absolute obedience and flawless performance. Therefore we each have in our personas negatives as well as positives.

For example, a person can be a chronic grouch (a trait most people would consider negative) and still be acceptable. A person can be short-tempered and still be acceptable. A person can be ruthless in business, while being honest and doing nothing illegal, and be acceptable. A person can demonstrate a "heart of stone" and be feelingless, and still be an acceptable personality.

Some may argue about the "acceptability" of such personalities, but such would be a highly subjective and personal argument. It could be equally argued that a great many of us possess these and similar "undesirable" traits and characteristics in our personas, perhaps to a lesser degree, and are quite aware of them and quite willing to maintain the status quo. Fortunately, the law of opposites holds true here: There are positive elements in the shadow that correspond to negative elements in the persona. Thus, a person with a persona element of short temper possesses the opposite shadow element of long-suffering or patience. The chronic grouch possesses the shadow attribute of potential cheerfulness. The feelingless person with a "heart of stone" possesses the shadow characteristic of potential empathy. These shadow attributes exist potentially in the same intensity and magnitude as their opposites exist in the persona.

Here we have our first glimpse of the Golden Shadow. It is certainly less familiar than the negative aspect of shadow. Comparatively little has been done to "publicize" the concretely positive elements in shadow and to encourage their discovery and use. That, essentially, is the purpose of this book, and the goal of our quest.

The darkness of shadow and its foreboding nature give little encouragement to entering it. Nevertheless, since shadow in its darkness is the first dimension that we encounter on our journey, we must explore that aspect, and realistically face the task and the choice that is always before us.

CHAPTER 2

The Journey Inward

A woman once told me in all sincerity that she had no shadow. It was during a retreat for married couples, where I had been speaking about the projection of shadow onto one's spouse in a marriage relationship; how it is imperative that we own our own dark side so that we do not unconsciously project it onto and accuse our spouse of our own shortcomings.

It was a Sunday afternoon in autumn. During the refreshment break this woman attending the seminar approached me at the coffee urn and pleasantly reported to me, "All this stuff about the shadow is very interesting and all, but I don't have a shadow. I would never *think* of doing such terrible things that you say I have the potential to do."

She was a pleasant and bright woman who appeared to me to be quite genuine and authentic in her declaration. Her statement was not atypical; most of us initially find shadow concepts to be interesting observations, but not necessarily applicable to ourselves.

Before I could respond, however, a man approached. He acknowledged my presence, but quickly said to the woman, "I'm going home now; I'll see you there," and turned and left. *Immediately* the woman's face changed from a pleasant smile to a scowl.

"That was my husband," she snarled. She was a slight woman, but feisty. As she spoke, she became quite animated.

I chuckled and started to say, "Yes, I gathered . . . " but those were the only words I got out.

"Do you know where he's going?" she interrupted.

"Well, he said he was going home . . . "

"Do you know what he's going to do?" she snapped.

"No."

"He's going home to watch that stupid football game. He's going home and sit down in front of that stupid television set and watch that stupid football game with a can of beer in his hand."

As she became more agitated, her animation increased and the volume of her voice rose steadily.

"I tell you I am sick and tired of his attachment to that stupid game and that stupid set. I call him to come to dinner and he calls back, 'Just another minute, honey.' I call him again, and I say, 'C'mon Harry, everything is on the table,' and he hollers back, 'Wait just a minute; I want to see this one more play.' "

By now she was speaking quite rapidly and loudly, so that others from the seminar standing nearby had stopped their conversations and were listening intently. The woman went on, oblivious to them.

"I say, "Harry! Will you come out here before everything is cold as ice!' And he yells back, "Yeah, I'm coming. I just want to see if they're going to kick or try to run it.' "

"I tell you," she said to me with a steel-cold voice and fiery eyes, "I tell you, one of these days I'm going into that living room and I'm going to take that can of beer out of his hand and I'm going to pour it over his head and smash that can down on his bald skull . . . "

She ended in mid-sentence, her voice loud and at high pitch, her arm poised over her head, clutching an imaginary beer can. Suddenly she had become aware that there was no sound in the room save *her* voice, and that all eyes were on her, gleefully observing her performance.

She turned red with embarrassment and began to shuffle her feet. She straightened up and smiled a Cheshire cat smile. She giggled a nervous laugh and by then the hubbub of conversation had resumed.

The "woman with no shadow" had just experienced her first conscious glimpse of the dark side. This small, gentle woman who shortly before told me she "would never *think* of doing such terrible things" had just heard herself plotting to assault her husband with the intent to do him physical harm.

THE DIFFICULTY OF FACING SHADOW

Some may discount such an account as this and dub it only a humorous anecdote that one should not take too seriously. "After all, people do tend to exaggerate things in colorful ways," they may say, and want to let it go at that. This kind of response is fairly typical of those who are afraid that there might just be some truth to it all for them and will therefore not allow it to have any veracity at all. They either laugh it off as something not to be taken seriously, or they become highly defensive and quite adamant in their denial of any shadow possibility within them.

And yet, if we are even slightly aware of ourselves, we know that experiences such as the above anecdote are far from rare. In fact, this turns out to be one of the clearest ways to identify our shadow's attributes—through slips of the tongue and slips of behavior. Any time we hear ourselves saying something we claim we would *absolutely never say*, we have come face to face with a facet of our personal shadow. Any time we experience ourselves doing something we have said we would *absolutely never do under any circumstances*, we have come face to face with another facet of our personal shadow.

These experiences are not uncommon occurrences to those who are aware of themselves. Since shadow is a part of us, it accompanies us wherever we go and is present in whatever we do. When Robert Louis Stevenson wrote the children's poem, "My Shadow," was it only a children's poem about the shadow that our body casts when we stand in the light? Or was it about the dark and hidden side—the shadow side—of our personality?

> I have a little shadow that goes in and out with me,
> And what can be the use of him is more than I can see.
> He is very, very like me from the heels up to the head;
> And I see him jump before me when I jump into my bed.
>
> The funniest thing about him is the way he likes to grow—
> Not at all like proper children, which is always very slow;
> For he sometimes shoots up taller like an India-rubber ball,
> And he sometimes gets so little that there's none of him at all.
>
> He hasn't got a notion of how children ought to play,
> And can only make a fool of me in every sort of way.
> He stays so close beside me, he's a coward you can see;
> I'd think shame to stick to nursie as that shadow sticks to me!
>
> One morning very early, before the sun was up,
> I rose and found the shining dew on every buttercup;
> But my lazy little shadow, like an arrant sleepyhead,
> Had stayed at home behind me and was fast asleep in bed.

Most of us know more about our shadow than we think we know or even want to know. Shadow taps us on the shoulder quite regularly, pressing for equal time on the stage. But we elbow our shadow back to where it belongs and smile broadly to the "audience," assuring them that we truly are what they see. But shadow persists and begins to push and shove, and we nervously kick and elbow it back into the wings or down the trap door into the dark room under the stage, tensely shouting out of the side of our mouth and over our shoulder (so the audience cannot see or hear), "Shut up, you devil, and get back down there. Do you want to ruin me?"If we do happen to glance over our shoulder and get a glimpse of this dark counterpart, we quickly snap our head back front and say, "I didn't see that."

Children watching a horror movie will cover their eyes at a particularly frightening scene. But their curiosity is so great that they will spread their fingers ever so slightly to get a shaded glimpse of the terrifying pictures on the screen. Likewise we and our shadows.

There is no point in hedging or trying to disguise the possible fear of entering into our shadow. It is both attractive and repulsive, inviting and frightening. Because our initial perception is more negative than positive, we are more highly motivated to put it off than to enter into the journey.

But it does not have to be that way. In this book, we will see it is possible to go beyond the negativity of the shadow, to discover and develop the gold hidden in the shadow—that is, to bring to the surface and exploit the underdeveloped and undeveloped potential in that hidden personality. We can even find gold in those undesirable and frightening dimensions by consciously using aspects of them in a positive and constructive way.

OUR RELUCTANCE TO LOOK INWARD

We are not alone in our reluctance to make the journey inward. In *The Archetypes and the Collective Unconscious*, psychiatrist Carl Jung describes a dream often dreamed by an unnamed Protestant theologian of his acquaintance:

[In the dream this man] stood on a mountain slope with a deep valley below, and in it a dark lake. He knew in the dream that something had always prevented him from approaching the lake. This time he resolved to go to the water. As he approached the shore, everything grew dark and uncanny, and a gust of wind suddenly rushed over the face of the water. He was seized by a panic fear, and awoke.*

*See Notes section on page 147 for full bibliographical information about sources quoted in this book.

The clergyman had dreamed this same dream many times. Each time was identical to the others. In the dream he has begun his journey inward, obviously in search. He has descended into the valley as he has numerous times before. In the past, however, he has gone only so far; he has stopped short of going further to the dark body of water. Since water is the universal symbol for the unconscious, we know that while the dreamer has apparently wanted (or has told himself he wanted) to enter into his unconscious for healing, for insight, for growth, he has stopped short each time. And it happens again. For in this dream, as in dreams past, he has become frightened and panicky because the experience suddenly becomes supernatural. Everything becomes dark, and a spiritual power rushes over the dark water; a power that is so real and spontaneous it spooks the dreamer, and he must flee by awakening.

Jung concluded that the dream is quite right in telling the man that down by the dark waters, foreboding as they are, he could "experience the working of the living spirit like a miracle of healing in the pool of Bethesda." But the dreamer was still reluctant to journey ahead.

In the same volume, Jung tells of another theologian who

dreamed that he saw on a mountain a kind of Castle of the Grail. He went along a road that seemed to lead straight to the foot of the mountain and up it. But as he drew nearer, he discovered to his great disappointment that a chasm separated him from the mountain, a deep darksome gorge with underworldly water rushing along the bottom. A steep path led downwards and toilsomely climbed up again on the other side. But the prospect looked uninviting and the dreamer awoke.

Moving into the unconscious for the sake of self-discovery is hard work, but it is rewarding. What will we find? Shall we take the risk? This dreamer saw the very desirable goal of the "shining height," the mountaintop, the peak. But to achieve the goal of ascending the mountain he had first to descend into the depths of the foreboding gorge and *then* climb the other side. It is a highly symbolic dream of the great quest.

This theme is repeated over and over in myths, legends, tales, and stories throughout the history of humankind. But people in general discount the significance of this great symbolism and believe the Grail may be won by a straight upward climb. This is particularly true of people in our Western culture, whose grail is only material with no spiritual interest; who *do* climb the mountain and reach the peak without having descended into the gorge. Many, however, find the victory strangely empty and unsatisfying.

The dreamer was a cautious, moderate, judicious man. He chose to play it safe. Prudence was the better part for him. Certainly no one may be critical of such a decision. After all, did we not learn early on that if we do not look out for our own neck, who will? Where do we find truth, wisdom, spirit, insight, knowledge, understanding? Is it not in the heights? What is in the depths but refuse, slime, disgust, rot? Mythically, the spirits soar overhead in the heights; demons inhabit the underworld. Light is up; darkness is down. Heaven is above; hell is the pits.

In the face of such overwhelming "evidence," it is not too difficult to understand the "reasonableness" of the dreamer's choice in his dream. Many, if not most of us human beings live under this great hoax that "enlightened" civilization has perpetrated for centuries. After all, as Nathanael said of Jesus, "What good thing could come out of *Nazareth?*" (John 1:46).

Nathanael was wrong; and the hoax is just that. Returning to the dream noted earlier, Jung says,

For people who think in this way [the way of the hoax], spirit means highest freedom, a soaring over the depths, deliverance from the prison of the chthonic world, and hence a refuge for all those timorous souls who do not want to become anything different. But water is earthy and tangible, it is also the fluid of the instinct-driven body, blood and the flowing of blood, the odor of the beast, carnality heavy with passion.

Gold is mined out of the earth and washed out of the water. To discover our Golden Shadow we lay prudence aside and journey into the unconscious; and our labors are not unrewarded. The surprise of discovery may be shocking, healing, and growth-producing.

A TREASURE IN AN UNLIKELY PLACE

Walter Hilton was a medieval English mystic whose writings help us toward an important understanding of the shadow. He was the Augustinian Canon of Thurgarton Priory near Southwell in Nottinghamshire, in the latter half of the fourteenth century. He produced several works of teachings on the spiritual life, the best-known of which is *The Scale of Perfection*. It is a "way book" or guide for the soul traveling in spirit toward union with God through contemplation. In a fascinating style, Hilton describes the necessity of journeying into the darkness and foreboding of the shadow. (I have taken the liberty to modestly modernize some of Hilton's fourteenth-century English.)

But what shalt thou find? Surely this: a dark and painful image of thine own soul which hath neither light of knowing nor feeling of love nor liking. This image, if thou behold it closely, is wrapped in black, stinking clothes of sin as pride, envy, ire, sloth, covetise, gluttony, and lechery.

This image and this black shadow thou bearest about with thee wherever thou goest. Out of this spring streams of sin, great and small . . . Out of this image spring stirrings of pride, of envy and so forth, the which cast thee down from the honesty of man into a beast's likeness. Peradventure thou beginnest to think within thyself what this image is like and I will tell thee. It is like no bodily thing. Truly it is nothing . . . This nothingness is nought else but darkness of conscience, a lacking of love and light; as sin is nought else but a wanting of God.

Nevertheless in this dark nothingness it behooveth thee to labor and sweat . . . And then when thou findest right nothing but sorrow and pain and blindness in this darkness, if thou wilt find Jhesu thou must suffer the pain of this dark conscience and abide a while therein . . . For within this nothingness is Jhesu hid in his joy, whom thou shalt not find with all thy seeking unless thou pass through this darkness.

Hilton makes a strong case for the wisdom of traveling into the unconscious shadow even though the journey is possibly fearsome and arduous. He says his express purpose in writing the book was to encourage the reader to do just this. His words are a hopeful promise. To know ourselves is finally to look inside—finally to explore the inner world instead of allowing ourselves to be continually inundated by the outer world. And in the process we will indeed make amazing discoveries. Those who seek the Lord will be unsuccessful in their search until they finally move into the depths of their being and own their shadow material. They will find him where, according to many principles of moral judgment and theological tenet, he would least be expected to be found.

This is true of much of our searching.

So we continue on to the "lake of dark waters," and we descend into the "darksome gorge with rushing underworldly waters," and we "labor and sweat in our dark nothingness." Where will we find our true self except in the depths of ourselves? Where else will we find our true selves, out of which we will ascend to the heights of true self-fulfillment?

We must, however, be motivated to make the move toward self-knowledge; one obviously does not do this simply for lack of anything better to do. The dreamer who decided not to descend into the gorge in order then to climb the mountain, concluded that the "prospect looked uninviting" and thus declined the experience. This is a typical response that is certainly more the rule than the exception. After all, who wants to leave the known for the unknown—to depart the comfort of the status quo to pursue what such a person might consider a will-o'-the-wisp? Why not let well enough alone (if it is indeed well enough), let sleeping dogs lie, and go about one's life in the usual fashion? Why open the door for possible pain when there is enough pain in life as it already is? If I am a good enough person, and even (and especially) if I am not, why tamper with my existence? Or in the current idiom, "If it ain't broke, don't fix it."

Who determines whether it is "broke" or not, however, is another matter.

WE MIGHT NOT BE THE BEST JUDGE OF OUR CONDITION

An interesting observation about mass surveys is that they are often inaccurate. The pollster can and does faithfully report how people respond to questions and statements, but the people responding may not be trustworthy. This is not meant to be critical, simply observational. For example, a popular subject for pollsters has to do with job satisfaction and related matters, not the least of which is financial remuneration for work performed. Polls seem to show consistently that many (if not the majority) workers claim that "more money" is not the basic issue in continued job satisfaction. Respondents may report that they prefer shorter hours, better health benefits, better retirement programs, extra holidays, longer vacations, and job security to increased salary.

A closer look shows these preferences to be both directly and indirectly nothing less than "more money." Furthermore, simply checking a box on a survey sheet is one thing; talking privately at length with an interviewer is something else again. In the privacy of the interview, respondents often disclose positions and attitudes other than those marked on the survey. Given some time to consider the matter more fully, it is not at all unusual for a person to conclude, "Hmmm; more money is more important than I thought. I hadn't looked at it that way." Possibly there is also an unconscious moral factor at work that discourages some people from checking the "more money" option for fear of appearing greedy and materialistic.

On a survey of job abilities and performance, many workers will grade themselves lower than objective accuracy would dictate. When allowed to discuss their abilities and performance with a pollster on a one-to-one basis, however, respondents tend to tell a more realistic story. An unconscious value may again be dictating that the respondents not describe themselves too highly for fear of being seen as or seeing themselves as arrogant braggarts.

The point is that, in determining whether or not we are "broke or not," we may not be the best diagnosticians. Too often we live too much of our lives rationalizing, avoiding and denying reality, pretending, building up thick personas, putting on a happy face, discounting losses, maintaining a hectic pace to avoid the threat of solitude. We convince ourselves that it isn't bad but it will get better; we look for the "big break" (that for many never comes); we wonder about our abilities (and often doubt them); we crave closeness but fear intimacy, and on and on.

It becomes clear rather quickly that most of us do not know ourselves nearly as well as we like to believe we do. There are certainly many things about us that confuse us. Many people can readily identify with the Apostle Paul when he complains, "I do not understand my own actions. For I do not do what I want, but I do the very thing I hate" (Rom. 7:15 RSV). Many people simply cannot put their finger on the issue or issues, but suffer that vague, undefined, indefinite sense of mental and moral ill-being called "malaise":

"What's the matter?"

"I don't know."

"Are you sick?"

"No. I may not be in perfect health, but that's not it."

"What is it then?"

"I don't know."

"Any major problems in your life?"

"No."

"Got any money problems?"

"Well, we could always use more, of course; but we're making it."

"Are you depressed?"

"Oh . . . no. I wouldn't say I was really depressed. No."

"Things OK with your spouse and kids?"

"Oh yeah, that's OK."

"How about the job?"

"Job's OK. Of course, everything could always be better down there, but it's OK."

"So you just feel 'yech,' eh?"

"Well . . . yeah."

"No real reason; you just feel 'yech.' "

"Right."

We usually look first for physical bases and medical solutions. Then possibly it is a neurosis (but we don't call these things neuroses any more). It could have sociological roots. It could even be a spiritual matter. It is none of these—and it is all of these. It is a sickness of the soul; it is a matter concerning one's whole being.

Little wonder that much of humanity should approach the elder years with a general and vague sense of incompleteness and lack of fulfillment embodied in those three, almost universal statements: "I did not take enough risks"; "I did not assert myself enough"; "I lacked self-discipline."

As is so often the case, the potential solution lies within the problem itself. The solution to our situation lies within us, in our Golden Shadow. But we have to make the journey inward in order to make our discoveries.

CHAPTER 3

The Benefits of Knowing Yourself

Much of this book has to do with risk-taking; and the greatest risk of all is to "know thyself." This exhortation is usually credited to Plato, but it seems to have appeared first inscribed on the temple of Apollo at Delphi. "Know thyself!" Thomas Carlyle wrote somewhat sarcastically, "Hence, too, the folly of that impossible Precept, *Know thyself;* till it be translated into this partially possible one, *know what thou canst work at.*"

Of course all things are relative, but there are at least five substantial benefits to journeying inward to "know thyself as best thou canst": to become more conscious, to become more authentic, to perceive the world truly, to accept ourselves as we are, and to discover our undeveloped self.

TO BECOME MORE CONSCIOUS

We journey inward to know ourselves so we may take better charge of our lives, act more consciously, and be less motivated and driven by unconscious needs, desires, and powers.

We can do nothing about that of which we are unaware. What is in the unconscious is, obviously, unconscious. If we are to do anything at all with such material, it is necessary for us to become aware of it, for only then are we able to be potentially outside its realm of power. I say potentially because once made conscious we have to choose what we will do with it—either resist, or identify with its good and evil and all shades in between.

Although the shadow is as much a part of us as is our persona, it is a stranger to us. It is such by its nature and by our choice. While others may hear and see manifestations of our "hidden side" ("Why can't he see how opinionated he is?"), we are compelled through selective hearing and vision to be ignorant of it ("I believe I am a very open-minded person!"). Thus it is that the shadow often surprises us and causes us no little amount of confusion, because our words or actions seem to be so opposed to what we believe about ourselves or think we know about ourselves. Many of us can easily identify with the Apostle Paul's words: "I do not understand my own actions!" (Rom. 7:15 RSV).

Fred, for example, had no idea of how strongly opinionated he was until he began his journey inward and sought feedback about himself from close friends. When two people who knew him well independently reported to him that they frequently saw him as narrow-minded and closed to others' opinions, he was shocked. "I certainly don't want to do that," he said. "In fact, that's the *last* thing I would want to be. I simply did not realize that I came across like that."

A powerful dimension of Fred's shadow personality manipulated his conscious personality without his even realizing it. He would never have identified himself as being strongly opinionated, but his close friends could see it clearly. Now that he was aware of this hitherto unknown dimension of himself, he was no longer simply being driven by this unconscious force. He could now choose to continue to consciously behave as he had before his new awareness; or he could choose to monitor his behavior and be less dogmatic and obstinate. Fred chose the latter and was delighted to discover how much more warm and accepting others were of him. It was frightening and embarrassing for Fred to become aware of this undesirable shadow trait. But the benefits of his new self-knowledge were well worth the pain of discovery.

Most of us do a fairly good job of running our lives. But from time to time our internal governors and gatekeepers fall asleep on the job and shadow pushes its way onto center stage embarrassing or even getting us into severe trouble. The more our shadow is a stranger to us, the more likely this is to happen. Therefore prudence and wisdom is to know ourselves, rather than to remain in blissful ignorance, comforted by the *seeming* prudence of avoiding the risk of self-knowledge.

The shadow is a formidable power, and we would do well to recognize that. If for no other reason than this we ought to know what it is that we are dealing with. In this book we deal mostly with the *personal* shadow, which by definition includes those traits, characteristics, attitudes, aptitudes, experiences, fantasies, and the like that have been repressed into the unconscious for personal reasons as one develops one's personality.

But beyond the personal shadow lies the *collective* shadow comprised mainly of material that is taboo to the larger culture and society in which one develops. What this culture itself disallows or expects provides the content of the collective shadow. For example, our culture has a taboo concerning incest, rage, and the using and abusing of others (especially women by men). It is the eruption of our collective shadow that frequently headlines the evening news.

The deepest level of shadow is the *archetypal* shadow, which is our natural inheritance by virtue of our humanity. It is the potential for horrendous evil, as well as the potential for unimaginable good that resides deeply and innately within every human being. The archetypal shadow adds power and energy to the personal and collective shadow. The archetypal shadow may empower a great philanthropic or self-sacrificing deed as well as the most horrendous crime imaginable. Not infrequently we read or hear of the horrors that some human beings inflict on other human beings as they act out the dreadful potential for evil in the archetypal shadow. Certainly the Nazi holocaust was fueled by the archetypal shadow.

Being aware of the dimensions of our shadow offers us the opportunity to control its activity. Shadow regularly presses for attention. We may naively believe that we have successfully gotten rid of all that was and is unacceptable to our subculture, but all we have done is suppress it into our unconscious where it lives its own existence and manipulates our lives as it will.

To know one's hidden self is to be able to do something about being in charge of it; not only to prevent its negative acting out, but to find a way to use it consistently in creative and constructive ways. We can be our own man or our own woman only when we have come to grips with the dynamic content of our shadow. Only then can we be truly positioned in the driver's seat of our lives.

TO BECOME MORE AUTHENTIC

We journey inward to know ourselves so we may become more authentic and genuine and less artificial as human beings.

"I was never aware of how much I was driven to being a people-pleaser," said Helen. "As I look back now, it's clear to me that I would go out of my way to be the 'perfect person' so people would like me."

As Helen moved into the second half of life, she began to become aware of rumblings of discontent within that frightened her. Little by little she discovered that much of her "public life" had been only a pleasant facade designed to offend no one and please everyone. "I think I have missed out on a lot of life by not allowing myself to be the self I truly was," she said. "But I never even realized until now that there was any other way. Being myself instead of always being 'Miss Perfect' surely does make life a lot easier and happier to live."

The development of personality is inevitably a compromise. Each of us wants to follow the path of least resistance in the process of development, but this, or course, is unallowable no matter what the subculture. Even in environments where morally reprehensible values are normative, such as in organized crime, there are parameters that one dare not cross. The more civilized the subculture, the greater the expectation for conformity by all its members. Thus the development of a persona is inevitable in the development of personhood.

Because of the element of compromise there is a degree of artificiality about the persona. Indeed the very word persona, signifying mask, implies that it is not the real thing, but is a false face covering the real thing. The real thing might be quite similar or dissimilar to the mask; no one really knows.

It is through my persona that I relate to the outer world, just as it is through my shadow that I relate to my inner world. Since in our general culture most of our psychic energy is focused outwardly and most of our dealings are outward bound, it stands to reason that each person's persona should become finely tuned in order that the person be as fully acceptable as possible to the subculture. The more heavily involved with the outer world we are, the more complex and varied is our persona. In fact, we may need several personas, each finely tuned to the various unique milieus to which we relate. This may become confusing, so that we may begin to wonder which is the real "I."

The greater danger, however, is to begin to identify with the persona and believe that we truly are what we appear to be, and nothing more. There is a narcissistic tendency within each of us to fall in love with what we appear to be, so it is not unusual for a person to fall prey to such a temptation. The identification with our persona is foolishly risky, because it causes us to become extremely vulnerable to being manipulated by our shadow. If I believe that I am only what I appear to be, then I am no more than that and I don't have to guard against shadow's antics because there *is* no shadow, inasmuch as there is nothing more to me than meets the eye.

To identify with our persona is to become two-dimensional and hence unreal. Many people with "model" personas appear unrealistically "good." We say of them that they are "too good to be true," and that classification is accurate because they are *not* true. They are false. People also identify with persona elements such as degrees, accomplishments, titles, or positions. People who do this are often quite hollow personalities; their inauthenticity is quite apparent. We say of them, "He is nothing more than his title"; "She is only her degree". "He is the accountant even in his shower." Just as others can see our shadow dimensions to which we ourselves are blind, so may they also "see through" the phoniness and artificiality we believe to be authenticity.

A certain amount of inauthenticity is unavoidable. But we know that the closer we live to the person we truly are (within the parameters of propriety) the more clearly we will know ourselves. This is not a kind of doubletalk. It is far too easy to fool ourselves into believing that we truly are whatever we *had* to appear to be. This causes only confusion and mixed identity and disallows embracing our true selves, which we must do if we are ever to move toward the experience of wholeness and completeness.

TO PERCEIVE THE WORLD TRULY

We journey inward to know ourselves so we may perceive the world as it is rather than as a projection of our shadow.

Jesus of Nazareth was given occasionally to overstatement; it was one of his most effective methods of teaching. Sometimes his statements make his point in such a ludicrous manner that they are actually funny. Quite possibly he did not intend these statements to be funny, but if we allow ourselves to savor the creative imagery, the humor is as evident as it the thrust itself. On one occasion (Matt. 19:23–24), after a disappointing encounter with a well-to-do man, Jesus commented, "I tell you, it will be hard for someone who loves his wealth to enter the kingdom of heaven. In fact, I would say it is easier for a camel to pass through the eye of a needle, than for a rich man to enter the kingdom of God."

On another occasion (Matt. 7:3–5), while talking to an assembly of listeners, he asked."Why is it that you see so very clearly the particle in your brother's eye but are completely oblivious to the log in your own eye? How can you go to your brother and say, 'Here, let me take that speck of sawdust out of your eye,' when you have a log sticking in your own eye? You hypocrite," he said, "first take the log out of your own eye and then you will see clearly to take the speck out of your brother's eye."

The easiest way to dispose of unwanted shadow material is to project it onto someone or something else. This fits nicely into our throwaway culture and society, but it has always been a part of the dynamic of human nature. Refusing to see and own a negative or undesirable trait or characteristic in ourselves, we throw (project) it onto another person and usually criticize that person for it. There must be a "hook" of sorts on that other person for the projection to stick, else it will simply slide off and be ineffective. If I wish, for instance, unconsciously to deny the presence of greediness in my shadow, it will do me no good to project it onto Mother Teresa, because it will not stick. If I begin to speak critically of Mother Teresa's greed, you will probably laugh and say to me, "Come now; you may possibly be critical of some aspects of Mother Teresa's behavior, but you simply cannot call her greedy."

I may, however successfully project the greediness of my shadow onto a local politician who has been advocating a tax increase. I can probably get away with saying, "I know him. He just wants to get more money into the city's coffers so he can get a pay raise." Political figures are excellent targets for shadow projections because they offer so many hooks.

Parents often "see" in their children undesirable traits and characteristics they refuse to see in themselves. Spouses project shadow elements onto each other. Workers project onto co-workers; neighborhoods onto neighborhoods; nations onto nations. There is, it seems, no end to the possibilities of projection and the distortion it may produce.

While projection is an easy and effective means of dealing with one's unconscious shadow elements, it is extremely undesirable because it generates a misinterpretation of the world around us. If we do not know our true selves we will not be able to distinguish reality from shadow projection. Human beings are generally more apt to give credence to a shadow projection than to reality. It is much more comfortable to criticize evil "out there" than to own it and confess it "in here."

Shadow projection is a powerful human dynamic. It is at the root of prejudice, judgment, discrimination, bigotry, rejection, and favoritism. Self-knowledge can begin to free us from its distorting power. People who make the journey inward almost universally declare how differently they see the world once they own their own shadow traits and stop projecting them on others. We begin to see people as they truly are, rather than as reflections of our own undesirable characteristics.

TO ACCEPT OURSELVES AS WE ARE

We journey inward to know ourselves so we may be able to accept ourselves as we are.

Because we tend to confuse self-knowledge with mere awareness of our conscious ego personalities, most of us mistakenly believe we truly know ourselves. Such superficial understanding, however, prevents our being able to capitalize on the breadth and depth of self that each of us is. Since self-acceptance is fundamental to self-development, we want to have the broadest base of self-understanding available to us. The better we know ourselves, the greater the potential to accept ourselves as we are.

Self-acceptance is fundamental to self-development because it provides much of the energy necessary to the process. Without the self-confidence that Patricia built through her growth in self-acceptance, for example, she would never have entered law school and became a fine lawyer. She believed that her "loose living," as she identified it, made her unworthy to pursue the profession she had always wanted. Her journey into her shadow provided not only the rediscovery of long-buried talent and interest in the legal profession, but also empowered her to move beyond her conscious shame and self-rejection. Her acceptance of her "unacceptable self" opened the door for her realization of unfulfilled potential.

Self-esteem is based on our ability to accept ourselves in our weaknesses as well as in our strengths, and in our successes and failures alike. Many people say they certainly can accept the positive dimensions of themselves, but they want to have nothing to do with the undesirable elements. The apostle Paul in his many letters to the young Christian churches strongly encouraged this practice (for example, Gal. 5:19 ff., Rom. 13:11–14; Eph. 5:2–20; Col. 3:5 ff.). This, however, causes people to be two-dimensional and less than real, and furthermore makes them vulnerable to the dark and evil potential within.

Some people believe that to accept is to condone or even to nurture. To accept is to take one as one is without judgment. This is how a counselor approaches each counselee in order to be helpful. Anything less is rejection, and no one who feels rejected by a person will be able to be helped by that person regardless of what that person says or does. We therefore approach ourselves in an attitude of acceptance even as we are accepted by our Creator.

Acceptance by God is a strong element in the journey inward, for that journey is, among other things, a spiritual journey. Some people fear rejection by God. They want to believe the truth of God's forgiveness, but fear that their sins place them beyond it. Others simply may not believe that God's grace is great enough to be extended to them. Envisioning, the powerful evil potential of their shadow compounds the anxiety, and they are keenly reluctant to journey inward.

All this notwithstanding, Hilton reminds us that this is precisely where the Lord is to be found, hidden in his joy.

This is perhaps too incomprehensible for the mind that reels at the possibility of there being anything at all good in what is so evil. But if Hilton is at all on track, seekers of Jesus will be unsuccessful and will continue to be unsuccessful as long as they seek him among the lilies. Jesus appears in the New Testament to have made his home among the "sinners"; therefore one ought not at all to be surprised by Hilton's announcement, but ought instead rejoice over its truth.

For here is the reality of grace most profound, so that it becomes far more than theological doctrine or dogma, and no one needs any further explanation or interpretation; for such a one has *felt* grace, and that is infinitely more powerful than any declaration. To own the darkness of ourselves and to know that we could perpetrate the most heinous of crimes—*and still in the face of it all feel the mercy of God*—is acceptance beyond intellectual comprehension. Thus if God our Creator accepts us as we are, certainly we can do no less than surrender to that acceptance and accept ourselves.

Only the journey inward can bring us to this profound awareness. Certainly a weekly recital of the prayer of general confession will not; nor will the inane observation, "No one's perfect."

TO DISCOVER OUR UNDEVELOPED SELF

We journey inward to know ourselves so we may be able to discover the underdeveloped and undeveloped self.

The purpose of this book is to encourage and help us mine the shadow's gold. For just as the shadow bears its dark, evil potential, so it bears the potential for great good and the positive resources for unrealized potential. The only way we know to capitalize on this is to take the risk of turning around and moving through the shadow into the inner world of our unconscious.

When we enter the shadow, it is invariably the dark, undesirable, evil potential that we first encounter. It is hardly flattering and may indeed be frightening. It is something that most of us will try to avoid for as long as we can successfully project our negative dimensions onto someone else. But as Walter Hilton has encouraged, we must "abide a while therein." This can be discouraging, and it is important that we not lose the hope and expectation of discovering true gold.

And there is gold to be had, even from these "black stinking clothes of sin," as Hilton describes it. We can find a way to bring that negative potential into contact with its counterpart in the persona and effect a unification of these opposites. Thus we find a way to use creatively and constructively what we loathed before or even wanted to deny the existence of within ourselves.

Furthermore, we discover the unconscious positive elements that are the counterparts of the nastiness in our conscious persona and work to bring about a unification of these opposites.

Beyond this lies the real gold of all the positive potential within us that never has had the opportunity to see the light of day. What treasures lie hidden in one's unconscious can be discovered only by the one who will seek them out.

Thus we conclude that the benefits of journeying inward to know ourselves are many, and the motivation may be strong indeed. The arguments to maintain the status quo are still present, but begin to show their underlying rationalizations. We slowly become convinced that there truly is no bliss in ignorance.

CHAPTER 4

Overcoming the Interference of the Outer World

In the myths, legends, and tales of "the great quest" theme, it is always necessary to surmount a series of obstacles before the quest can be successfully completed and the object of the quest is won. Our quest for the Golden Shadow is no exception. We, too, have obstacles to surmount and hurdles to clear on our journey inward to the Golden Shadow. The major obstacle we face is the interference and influence of the outer world. Most of us develop in an environment that is not only not conducive to looking inward, but may actually discourage or even forbid such behavior.

Imagine, if you will, young Bobby sitting quietly in his room, simply looking at the wall, rather void of expression. Mama enters and asks, "What are you doing, honey?"

"Nothing."

"Yes, dear, I can see that; but what are you doing?"

"Just thinking."

"But it's such a beautiful afternoon, why don't you go out and play with the kids?"

"I'd rather just sit here."

"Billy is working on that model airplane in the garage; why don't you go help him?"

"I don't want to."

"What are you thinking about?"

"I guess I'm sort of contemplating."

"Bobby, do you feel all right?"

"Yeah, I'm OK."

"Let me feel your forehead; do you have a temperature?"

"No, I'm fine."

"Are you tired, is that it?"

"No, I'm not tired."

"Well, I just don't understand."

"Understand what?"

"Why anyone would want to just *sit* here doing nothing!"

When mama speaks with daddy later in the day she will be sure to report this incident and possibly suggest that they take Bobby to the doctor to determine if there isn't indeed something physically wrong. After all, no healthy, red-blooded, developing boy should want to sit quietly in his room "contemplating" when he could be outside romping with his fellows, or working on a model airplane with his brother, or doing *something*.

For most of us the outer world is virtually all that we know; the inner world has never been a very vital part of our experience. It is a true stranger. Few of us realize how powerful the influence of the outer world has been and continues to be on our development. It is therefore important and necessary that we review this issue, so we may be as realistic and practical as possible in our quest.

We need first to return to our map of the psyche for just a moment and recall psyche's function as the dynamic connector of our outer and inner worlds. These are the two major sources that provide learning and serve as realms of experience: the inner world and the outer world. The task of one's psyche is somehow to bring these two together and help us relate to each.

At birth there appears to be no difference between the two; we are blessed with that marvelous egomania, which allows each of us to believe that I and the universe are one. Only as we grow into self-consciousness are we confronted with the rudeness of truth that there is an "outer world" that must be faced, listened to, and obeyed. For here in the outer world of subculture and larger culture is where we get our needs met and our wants fulfilled. This outer world seems to demand all our attention as we develop our personalities. It is there that we will be not only occupied, but will become preoccupied; and it is there that many of us will remain preoccupied for many years, if not for our entire lifetime, unless some intervention alters the pattern.

The outer world is the realm of tangible and material experience. It is all that comes to us through our bodily senses. It is all that is observable here and now in time and space. It is the logical and the rational—the realm of physics and mathematics. It is the realm of substance—the concrete. It seems perfectly reasonable that we should live in this world.

The inner world is the realm of the personal and collective unconscious—the realm of nonmaterial phenomena. It is that which is perceived in an extrasensory fashion. It is the realm of intuition—"seeing around the corner." It is the irrational; that which is spiritual; dreams, visions, daydreams, and fantasies. We wonder about the value of this world in our "real" lives.

It is clear that we are profoundly influenced by our outer world, which makes it all the more difficult to consider and to act on exploring our inner world. Even though the magnitude of the inner world far exceeds that of the outer world, most of us who develop in the Western hemisphere learn precious little from it, but are overwhelmingly influenced by our outer world.

THE VASTNESS OF THE INNER WORLD

How can I claim that the potential magnitude of what resides deeply within us is far greater than our outer world? After all, we are inundated every day by the outer world. Many of us are hardly aware of an inner world, let alone prepared to acknowledge it as far more vast than the tangible world in which we exist. Given what we have come to call the "knowledge explosion," is this not rather naive, unsophisticated thinking?

Unfortunately, this attitude is one of the major roadblocks to any journey inward. We become convinced that everything is "out there" and there is precious little "in here." We lose sight of the fact that none of us simply steps into history at the moment of our birth and begins fresh at that point. Rather, we bring with us a trace of all the experience of humanity before us; and that is overwhelming to consider.

We pick up an acorn, and as we study it realize that it contains the embodiment of millions of years of experience. Each generation of oak tree has passed on to its offspring all that it received from its ancestors—all the way back to the beginning. Likewise, every child born possesses all the "residues of ancestral life," as Jung refers to it, and the "repository of humanity's experience" all the way back to the beginning. This inner world's contents are virtually unfathomable, and their potential is beyond our wildest imagination. Little wonder that researchers and scientists consistently remind us that human beings hardly begin to tap their potential in their lifetimes. The presence of the inner world is there for each of us in far greater magnitude than is the presence of the outer world. Nevertheless, it is to the encounter with the outer world that most of us will devote our time and expend our energy.

To distinguish between East and West regarding this matter no longer presents the fairly clear-cut difference it once provided. We used to observe, and rightly so, that a primary difference between the Westerner and the Easterner was outward versus inward orientation. Orientals were seen as meditative, introspective, even mystical. Since World War II that difference has been gradually erased, because the technological permeation of Eastern culture is as pervasive there as in the West. Technologization and "modernism" have pushed aside much of that dimension, so that Orientals have become as outer world-oriented as Occidentals. As early as 1960, after a two-year "pilgrimage" through India and Japan, Arthur Koestler sardonically wrote, "To look to Asia for mystic enlightenment and spiritual guidance has become as much of an anachronism as to think of America as the Wild West."

THE MAGNITUDE OF OUTER WORLD INFLUENCE

In our journey inward, two significant observations become apparent: (1) We realize how strongly the outer world (our culture and subculture) has influenced the development of our personalities. (2) We realize how readily we focus virtually all our energy on the outer world, to the exclusion and detriment of exploring and cultivating the inner world.

It is reasonable to expect a greater occupation with the outer world, for there is where all the action is. There is the great trading counter where I connect with the many "Not I" and "That Other" elements of my subculture and culture. It is there that I bring up my traits, characteristics, attitudes, and aptitudes for consideration and evaluation. It is there that I must discover what is expected and required of me, so that I may develop it and thus be accepted, so I may get my needs met and my wants fulfilled. This is most important to me in my process of development.

Out of our vast inner storehouse we draw up and posit qualities that satisfy the expectations and demands of the outer world. We automatically reject the opposite of that quality, and it therefore remains in the unconscious. Personality, then, is developed largely to suit the expectations of the outer world.

It is difficult to determine to what extent we develop our own personalities as children. Undoubtedly, it is very little; for our subculture is filled with powerful adult figures who overtly and covertly impose their wills on us. An old Jesuit maxim says, "Give me a child for the first six years of life, and he'll be a servant of God till his last breath." The influence of the outer world on the developing personality is overwhelming. As any adolescent can attest, to develop a trait or characteristic other than those expected by the outer world involves meeting with considerable opposition, conflict, and stress. But it is through this process that we are necessarily "civilized," educated, and cultured.

The person that we develop into, then, is hardly the person that we would have chosen to develop into. Certainly, as we mature in years, we become more and more self-conscious and may bring up traits and characteristics we choose ourselves. But the essential building blocks of personality have already been laid.

No one can quarrel with the need to focus attention on development in relation to the outer world. Certainly we need to learn how to live in our environment, how to be accepted so we may survive, how to get along with people, how to make a living. The question should never be, shall we abandon outer concentration for inner, or vice versa. That is, however, how it appears to have become. We have over-nourished our affair with the outer world and starved our experience with the inner. There is no balance.

EXTRAVERSION IS THE STANDARD

The psychological terms introversion and extraversion have become household words to most of us. They have to do with how we generally tend to direct our energies—outwardly or inwardly. Introverts direct more of their energy inward and are more "private" and quiet. Extraverts direct more of their energy outward and are more gregarious and action-oriented.

Most of us grow up in an environment that is not only not conducive to looking inward, it may actually discourage or forbid such behavior. Western society in general strongly encourages, supports, and rewards extraversion, but only grudgingly tolerates or possibly even punishes introversion. After all, it is said, human beings are social beings and therefore ought to be gregarious, companionable, and congenial—it is our nature. Children are prompted to be "outgoing," to be sociable, to mingle with others. We ought to be doing something rather than "sitting contemplating" (as though sitting contemplating were doing nothing). We go so far sometimes as to dislike introvertive people. They are standoffish; because they "keep to themselves" they are considered snooty and unfriendly; and they are often under suspicion because they "must be hiding something."

Furthermore, extraversion is "the American way." It would require an extraordinary stretch of the imagination to perceive Uncle Sam as an introvertive type. The American is much more "hail-fellow-well-met" than contemplative.

Given all this, it is not difficult to recognize the little scenario at the beginning of this chapter as a realistic dialogue between mother and young son rather than a caricature. How difficult it will be for Bobby to develop as an introvertive personality is obvious. There will be pressure—strong pressure—from his subculture and the larger culture to reverse his personality inclination and conform to the standards. Bobby will either capitulate, develop a thick persona of extravertive qualities, and relegate his introvertive traits, characteristics, attitudes, and aptitudes to his unconscious shadow realm; or he will remain true to his natural self, undoubtedly at great cost, and struggle to be an "accepted" person.

One can certainly argue the *necessity* of outward orientation, and do so with a degree of reasonableness. But that is a truism, and is not the issue. Our concern has to do with the degree of the influence of the outer world on the developing personality and the ramifications of that influence. How much creativity and potential is squelched by such a procrustean milieu and consequently relegated to the unconscious, possibly to be lost to consciousness forever, is anybody's guess.

THE DEARTH OF INNER-WORLD INFLUENCE

Most of us mature in a subculture and culture that is not at all conducive to inner world dealings. Most of us are surrounded and inundated by the outer world most, if not all, of our waking hours. Our larger culture appears to have become addicted to the ever-presence of sound. There is "music" in public transportation vehicles, shopping malls, department stores, restaurants, elevators, in telephone systems. The addiction seems so great than some people must carry their own sound system with them wherever they go, just in case the environment should happen to be quiet. The louder and faster-paced the sound, the better able it is to distract us from ourselves. Either rightly or wrongly, some people define today's music as more noise than music. Some question whether it isn't injurious to the ears.

Radio and television announcers talk very rapidly, packing as many words as can be audibly discernable into fifteen-second commercials. "Dead air" is taboo, economically and culturally. We appear almost unable to tolerate silence and solitude. It annoys us; it possibly even frightens us.

In this milieu, the silence and the inward-looking nature of introspection may be downright intolerable. I was invited one time to speak to a statewide group of professionals, mostly counselors from social service agencies with denominational affiliations. One man had been asked by the sponsors to present a short devotional to open the morning session. His presentation was helpful and to the point. He made the "mistake," however, of including a moment of silent meditation wherein we were to do some self-examination. After about fifteen seconds of silence, someone coughed; then another. Then there was the shuffling sound of body movement—legs crossing, uncrossing, recrossing. A chair leg scraped the floor. The nonverbal message from the audience was, "Enough of this; let's get on with it, shall we?"

THE IMPACT OF TECHNOLOGY

The technologization of our culture has removed us most profoundly from inner world communication. Technologization displaces the primitive, and the primitive is essential to balance our sophistication and enable our communication with the inner world. But technological advancement is highly desirable because of the many positive advantages it provides us. Certainly few of us would complain about the convenience of modern travel and long to return to the horse and buggy. Few would want to abandon the marvels of computers and return to the comptometer and slide rule. Communication technology has made the world a "global village."

But all of this has not been without its price. Along with the mechanization and technologization in culture comes the mechanization and depersonalization of people. Unless there is a deliberate move to cultivate inner world dimensions in tandem with outer world technologization, depersonalization will occur. Technology will take us further and further away from our roots in the primitive—away from the groundedness of our being. For we are of the earth; we belong to the earth. The earth is our mother. To forget that is to forget our humanity. It is to disassociate ourselves from that which is far more us than the outer trappings imposed by the environment. Without appropriate balance, we endanger ourselves. As far as psyche is concerned, technological excesses often mean humanitarian deficits.

The power and influence of the outer world is great; the journey inward difficult. In the next chapter we will review several methods or "pathways" for journeying into the shadow. These pathways are clear and effective, but the influence and interference of the outer world are formidable obstacles to reaching our goal.

We are not without a resource, however for clearing this hurdle. One of the most effective methods for overcoming the interference and influence of the outer world is the discipline of meditation. Meditation can effectively push aside the interference of the outer world and facilitate entry into the inner world. But meditation demands time for the inner self; and that, of course, is a rude deviation from our normal course.

We have allowed the demands of modern living to reinforce our preoccupation with the outer world and to cause our perception to be that time has shrunk—we have progressively less and less of it. Very few people will quarrel with this, for it has become another badge of distinction in an outer world-dominated culture. The more profoundly we can say, "I have simply run out of time," the more honored and respected we are in that culture. Those who do not bemoan that fact may be considered "marginal." Therefore, to consider meditation as a discipline is precisely accurate; for it does require time, and time is what we say we do not have, and must necessarily discipline ourselves to find.

THE RESOURCE OF MEDITATION

The renewal of interest in meditation may be the result of a possibly intuitive need to compensate for the progressive technologization of our society. Perhaps some of us can tolerate the inundation of the outer world only so long, and then we must somehow find balance from the relatively unknown inner world. We cannot let the spiritual dimension of our being remain untended indefinitely and still expect to be whole and complete people.

While most futurists expect the focus to be on space travel, robots, "artificial intelligence," and other technological achievements, at least one predicts that the next decade will see a renaissance of spirituality, art, and literature. John Naisbitt, author of *Megatrends*, looks more for cultural changes. Naisbitt believes that people are more and more seeking to regain balance by reexamining and experiencing their humanity. Science and technology alone do not answer the question of life's meaning.

We have observed that the journey inward is, among other things, a spiritual journey; and, meditation is essentially a spiritual process. The dimension of spirituality is fundamental to the inner world. At the very core of our beings resides the Spirit of God. It is God who is at the base of that inexhaustible reservoir of humanity's experience, out of which we develop our personality and into which we journey on our quest. St. John reminds us of the absolute creativity of God when he declares, "Through him all things were made; without him nothing was made that has been made" (John 1:3 NIV). When, on one occasion, people asked Jesus about the coming of the kingdom of God he replied, "The kingdom of God does not come visibly, nor will people say, 'Here it is,' or 'There it is,' because the kingdom of God is *within you*" (Luke 17:20–21 NIV).

Thus, as we move inward, we draw on that inexhaustible resource: the power and support of God within us. We open ourselves to it and pray that God will help us to perceive what is there for us to gain. As we meditate we allow ourselves to lay aside all outer influences and focus only within ourselves. Meditation is simply a very personal discipline that helps us exclude the outer world and facilitate communion within. It is designed to encourage and allow us to focus intently on ourselves without external distraction, and without the need to be occupied with anything other than our concentration on ourselves.

This strong focus on ourselves heightens self-awareness and encourages us to pay conscious attention to the unconscious as it offers its hidden material. In the normal rounds of daily activity, preconscious and unconscious material has little or no access to our awareness because the external world necessarily demands our attention and interest. In a meditative state, when we are focused solely on self, this material becomes considerably more accessible.

REMOVAL FROM THE OUTER WORLD

An example of this sometimes occurs quite spontaneously when we are injured or become seriously ill and require hospitalization. We become intently focused on ourselves and tend to lay aside, at least temporarily, matters of the outer world. This is particularly true as we lie in the hospital bed, in treatment, anticipating surgery, or in recovery.

During this period of appropriate egocentricity and heightened self-awareness, we tend to become much more aware of matters and issues of which we were barely aware during good health. Because of the often hectic busyness of everyday living, we simply glossed over or denied and repressed those matters and issues, we had no time to deal with them, we had more important things to concern us, or we simply would not be aware of them. We were preoccupied with the outer world. But now that the pace has been slowed considerably, things "catch up with us." We find ourselves confronted by many of these matters and issues, which are *now* quite conscious and wanting attention.

Much of my ministry to hospital patients has been to help them deal with the sometimes disturbing insights about themselves that have come about as a result of the heightened self-awareness brought on by hospitalization. A man once told me how his hospitalization had "made him aware" of his dissatisfaction with his job, and how disappointed he was with himself for having done nothing about it for years and years. Technically, the hospitalization had not brought him to awareness; it had simply provided an opportunity and an atmosphere for what we might call "forced meditation." His preoccupation with the outer world (work and activities) had successfully insulated him from his shadow attitude of dissatisfaction; it disallowed his getting too close to himself—perhaps it *protected* him from getting too close to himself.

A retired sixty-five-year-old woman named Marie had extensive surgery, all of which was successful. Her lengthy hospital stay provided her time to do some "real soul searching"—or to meditate.

Marie's soul-searching had brought to memory a long-repressed desire to be a deaconess in her church. "I was amazed," she said, "that I had completely lost track of that; until suddenly, yesterday afternoon, lying here alone, it came to me. I've thought about hardly anything else since then. I'm afraid that it's too late for that now; but I have decided to look into becoming a hospital volunteer once I'm up and around."

Marie's wish to be a deaconess as a young woman centered around her interest in religion and in helping people. Her family situation prevented her from receiving the training necessary for such a position, so she abandoned the idea and relegated it to her shadow because it had no future in outer world dealings. She went on, instead, to become a secretary. Then one day, forty-five or more years later, when Marie "had the time" to "search her soul," she encountered her Golden Shadow, which yielded up a meaningful occupation for her in her retirement.

THE PROCESS OF MEDITATION

The process of meditation is not difficult. The most important ingredient is really not an actual ingredient at all, but rather allows for meditation to occur: the discipline of providing time to do it. Right up front is where we must come to grips with the powerful and demanding influence of the outer world and make our stand.

In the process of meditation there are essentially four simply elements: (1) a quiet environment, (2) a comfortable position, (3) a passive attitude, and (4) an object or a mental device on which to focus attention.

A QUIET ENVIRONMENT

A quiet environment, as free from distraction as possible, is necessary for effective meditation. In time, one acquires the ability to meditate at virtually any time and in any place: jogging, riding the bus, while waiting for an appointment or service. Initially, however, and particularly for our purpose here, it is desirable that a quiet environment be available. After all, we are engaging in a radical deviation from our norm of fixation to the outer world; therefore, we should seek all the help we can get.

A COMFORTABLE POSITION

There is no "best" position in which to meditate; it is quite a personal matter. One should be comfortable, but not too comfortable. Generally, it is helpful to sit upright on a straight-back chair, keeping the spine erect, with both feet on the floor and with hands placed on the thighs. We want to be comfortable so there is no distraction due to pains, cramps, numbness, or ache-producing posture; but not so comfortable that we drop off into sleep.

The state of meditation lies between the state of sleep and the state of active involvement with our environment. Initially, at least, drowsiness can be a problem, particularly if we begin to become aware of personal material from the unconscious that we are not ready or willing consciously to deal with. Going to sleep has long been enjoyed as an effective escape from the undesirable, and a mechanism of defense from the intolerable. We ought not become discouraged by the experience of drowsiness, because it does assure us that we have become successfully relaxed, and that *is* a goal of meditation. In time, as meditation becomes more a part of our experience, this matter tends to be less of an issue.

A PASSIVE ATTITUDE

In meditation, we face another radical opposite from our experience with the outer world—a passive attitude. We relax and let it happen, having no concern about whether we are doing it "right," or how successful we will or will not be. Physical relaxation is of great importance. We relax our muscles, beginning with our toes, our feet, up through calves, knees, thighs, back, shoulders, upper arms, elbows, forearms, wrists, fingers, neck, jaw, and face. In this state of relaxation, we may experience ourselves as feeling very light, such as floating on air or in salt water.

A FOCUS OF ATTENTION

The focus of attention in meditation varies according to personal preferences; it is usually a matter of what works best. The purpose of focusing is to help further the process of turning away from the outer world and turning inward. One may possibly focus on an object, a feeling, a phrase or word, or oneself. For example, Herbert Benson and Miriam Klipper, in *The Relaxation Response*, suggest simply repeating silently the word, "one," in connection with deep breathing. Others recommend fixed gazing at an object. William Hulme, in *Let the Spirit In*, encourages focusing on our bodies—that is, our lungs (breathing) and abdomen (digestion). This latter recommendation seems best for our purpose, for our intent is to focus on ourselves— that is the point of our concentration—to allow us to journey into ourselves for our discoveries.

We close our eyes and begin to breathe deeply from the abdomen, taking a long, slow inhalation to the count of four, holding it to the count of two, and exhaling it slowly to the count of four. Paying close attention to the breathing and the counting, we do this inhalation-exhalation about fifteen times. In this meditative state we are at the threshold of the inner world.

Meditation is an excellent vehicle to facilitate our journey inward. In the ensuing chapters we will consider specific applications of meditation to the various aspects of our journey. For example, chapter five outlines several methods for gaining insight into one's personal shadow. Meditation can be a very helpful tool to aid us in this examination. Meditation can also help bring to consciousness our undeveloped and underdeveloped potential. Through the help of meditation we may enhance our self-image and build up our self-esteem. The power of imaging and visualizing in meditation will support our work as we deal with the matters of risk-taking and failure. Meditation can promote and encourage creativity, and provide a powerful support to living out our plans and dreams.

CHAPTER 5

Pathways into the Shadow

After twenty years of marriage, Alice and her husband separated and then divorced. The divorce had been final for over a year, and now Alice felt a strong need to know and understand herself more intimately. "I believe I'm ready to journey into my shadow," she said, "and I want to do it. But I need help, and I know I'm going to need support."

I told Alice that there are several ways to become acquainted with our shadow; but it would be well to consider, first of all, enlisting a "traveling companion" to join her on her journey inward. As she intuitively surmised, the journey is rather arduous, at least at the beginning, and it is important to have someone else know what we are about. The "someone else" may be a therapist or counselor, a professional person who understands the psych's workings; or a trusted and loyal friend who knows the traveler well and agrees to "walk with" the traveler on the journey. The companion should be neither a leader (guide) nor a follower, but one who will walk alongside, hand-in-hand. The companion should be a person who will accept and be nonjudgmental; who will not criticize, give advice, or refuse to take seriously the ramblings of the traveler.

The journey inward can, of course, only be made alone. The reason for the companion on this lonely journey is to provide support, encouragement, and empathy—to commiserate and celebrate with the journeyer; to act as a leveler, a sounding board, a mirror; to lend perspective; to provide feedback. The companion performs a "ministry of presence."

When we have chosen a person whom we believe would adequately fulfill the requirements of traveling companion, we tell that person what we are about—what we plan to do on our journey, and where we hope to arrive in terms of fulfilling our potential self. We tell the person what we expect and need in a traveling companion and ask if he or she would be willing to meet with us regularly during at least the initial portion of the journey inward to provide the kind of companionship we need.

Sometimes religious people wish to argue that it is sufficient to have God at our side and therefore unnecessary to have another human being. Having the spirit of God with us is by all means desirable and helpful; but on the journey inward the traveler needs flesh and blood as well—a gentle voice, accepting eyes, a loving face, physical touch.

There are at least five effective pathways for traveling inward to gain insight into the composition of our shadow: (1) soliciting feedback from others as to how they perceive us; (2) uncovering the content of our projections; (3) examining our "slips" of tongue and behavior, and investigating what is really occurring when we are perceived other than we intended to be perceived; (4) considering our humor and our identifications; and (5) studying our dreams, daydreams, and fantasies.

SOLICITING FEEDBACK FROM OTHERS

We may begin by looking *beyond* the mirror at our own reflection. Looking into a mirror we see only the reflection of ourselves as we choose to see it. Looking beyond the mirror we see ourselves *as we are seen*. If this seems impossible, begin with someone else.

Bring to mind the image of a person whom we know to live to some degree in self-delusion. This is not difficult, because we are all too familiar with the shadow dimensions of other people, and we are often amazed that they are so ignorant of what is so obvious.

Even though I may *want* to deny it, I am compelled to agree (at least in theory) that this matter is a two-way street. That is to say, if I can see clearly your shadow to which you are blind, then it must follow that you likewise can see clearly my shadow to which I am blind. If I would be more than happy to tell you what I see (in a nice way, of course), then you would probably be more than happy to tell me what you see (in a nice way, of course).

This is one of the most effective methods for gaining insight into our personal shadow—feedback from others as to how they perceive us. Unfortunately, the very thought of this is threatening to most of us. We would much rather continue to assume that others see us precisely as we see ourselves. But once on the journey into self we can no longer enjoy this luxury, else we will sabotage the venture in its first quarter-mile.

Students who come into a formal training program to learn how to minister to people in a critical setting usually make a pact with their supervisor and peers to give them feedback regarding how they are perceived by these colleagues. Their stated goal is the desire to gain insight into themselves so they may deal consciously with those personal dynamics that may hamper their effective ministry. It is certainly an admirable learning goal.

More often than not, however, "the spirit is willing but the flesh is weak." Most students truly believe that they want critical feedback from supervisor and peers: but when it is actually given, students frequently become defensive, argumentative, and accusatory. It matters not how firmly the feedback can be grounded in empirical evidence. The observation made by the colleague may be simply too much for the student to "hear," so it is rejected. The student may actually resent the colleague for giving the feedback. It seems, in fact, that the more grounded in empirical evidence the feedback is, the more threatened and defensive the recipient becomes. All this, of course, in spite of the fact that this is precisely what the student requested in the first place.

This is simply to remind us before we move too far into this task that to decide on a course of action in the comfort of our armchair is one thing: to experience that course of action on the "dusty road of life" may be something else again.

But we need not be discouraged; such a reaction is certainly not abnormal. As a supervisor of such students I have heard hundreds respond initially in this manner. In time they realize that what we are about requires that defenses be laid down and courage raised up if insight is to be had. As the supervisor learns to be patient with students, so we learn to be patient with ourselves. In fact, an immediate, unqualified "acceptance" of critical feedback would cause one to wonder about its sincerity.

People who are in the best position to help us see our shadow elements are those who know us well. It could be our spouse, significant other, close friend, colleague, or fellow worker. Paradoxically, the people who are most likely to be helpful are those whom we are least likely to heed. We may accuse them of overt subjectivity, projection, or just plain fabrication. It would be less threatening to hear feedback from a stranger, but strangers are not in the position to give us the kind of authentic perceptions as are those who know us well. It is yet another indication of the difficulty of the journey.

Louise and Jerry had been married thirty years. They had both begun their journeys inward and depended on each other to provide primary feedback to the other regarding perception of shadow traits. Both knew it would be difficult to hear and accept the other's feedback without becoming defensive. To overcome the possibility of rejecting the other's feedback, they agreed that each could "blow the whistle" on the other if the other became defensive. For example, if Jerry became defensive, Louise would interrupt him, remind him of their pact, and tell him to stop talking defensively and consider the feedback she was giving him. In this manner each was compelled to receive what each had requested of the other.

In this process of gaining insight into our personal shadow it is important to seek a second or third opinion. Projections can occur and misperceptions are always possible. While on the one hand we do not want to write off an unflattering observation as a projection of the observer, neither do we want to accept every shred of feedback unquestioningly.

Suppose I solicit your feedback, and you tell me that you have perceived me as a condescending person in several situations in which we have both been involved. I may accept that as your valid observation, even though it is difficult for me to hear. I want to say, "What on earth are you talking about? That is the *last* thing I want to be—condescending." But I hold my tongue.

This gives me a fairly substantial clue that I probably have just met a true shadow trait or characteristic. For anytime we overstate being "for" or "against," and press that position adamantly, we may just be in personal shadow territory, and we would do well to investigate.

I have heard your identification of my shadow trait, and even though I find it extremely hard to believe that I should appear to be condescending, I accept it as your perception. I then go to a close friend and explain to him what I am doing and tell him that another friend has told me that she sees me as a condescending person. I ask him to be honest and tell me if that is how he has perceived me. I may be satisfied with this second opinion, or I may want to repeat this process again. In any case, if I am sincere in my journey inward, I will want to know as best I can, one way or the other. When two or more people independently tell me they perceive in me a common shadow trait, I would do well to believe them and explore more deeply their observation.

One of the most significant ways to realize the content and nature of our shadow is in our human relationships. Others frequently give us feedback regarding how we present ourselves. If we but listen to them and take to heart their comments, we will come to a recognition of many shadow dimensions. By and large, people neither maliciously nor willy-nilly make up "charges" against us. Much more often than not, there is real validity to what they have to say. If we can move past the immediate threat to our ego and deny ourselves the need to put down the critic, we can learn much about our hidden selves from the gentlest confrontation to the harshest criticism.

EXAMINING OUR PROJECTIONS

A second pathway into the personal shadow is to examine our projections. Projection is an unconscious mechanism that is employed whenever a trait or characteristic of our personality that has no relationship to consciousness becomes activated. As a result of the unconscious projection, we observe and react to this unrecognized personal trait in other people. We see in them something that is a part of ourselves, but which we fail to see in ourselves.

We make both negative and positive projections. Most of the time, however, it is the undesirable dimensions of our selves that we see in others. Therefore, to encounter the elements of the shadow, we need to examine what traits, characteristics, and attitudes we dislike in other people and how strongly we dislike them.

The simplest method is to list all the qualities we do not like in other people; for instance, conceit, short temper, selfishness, bad manners, greed, and others. When the list is finally complete (and it will probably be quite lengthy), we must extract those characteristics that we not only dislike in others, but hate, loathe, and despise. This shorter final list will be a fairly accurate picture of our personal shadow. This will probably be very hard to believe and even harder to accept.

If I list arrogance, for example, as one of those traits in others that I simply cannot stand, and if I adamantly criticize a person for arrogance in relating to people, I would do well to examine my own behaviors to see if perhaps I, too, practice arrogance.

Certainly not all our criticisms of others are projections of our own undesirable shadow traits: but any time our response to another person involves excessive emotion or overreaction, we can be sure that something unconscious has been prodded and is being activated. As we said earlier, the people on whom we project must have "hooks" on which the projection can stick. If Jim is sometimes arrogant, for example, there is a certain degree of "reasonableness" about my offense at his behavior. But in true shadow projection my condemnation of Jim will far exceed his demonstration of the fault.

Conflict situations generate many issues and bring forth strong emotions; consequently, they provide an exceptional arena for possible shadow projections. In the experience of conflict we may be able to learn much about our shadow characteristics. What we decry in the "enemy" may be nothing less than a shadow projection of our own darkness.

We also project our positive shadow qualities onto others: We see in others those positive traits which are our very own, but which, for whatever reason, we refuse to allow entry into our consciousness and are undiscernible to us.

For example, we may perceive positive qualities in people without empirical evidence to support such perceptions. This often happens in romantic encounters and sometimes in personnel evaluations. Lovers, caught up in their desire for the other person, often project their own unconscious positive attributes onto that person. The trait projected may in fact be there in some form, else the projection will not stick. But frequently it is there nowhere to the degree that the other believes he or she sees it. For example, Susan, who possesses a very kind and generous dimension in her shadow, projects it onto Sam and lauds him for his great kindness, particularly to her. Friends may try to help Susan see that while Sam may not appear to be selfish and greedy, his demonstrations of kindness and generosity are more like "flashes in the pan." Susan, however, will hear none of this.

When one is once "hooked" by a positive quality in another person, one may project all sorts of other positive qualities onto that person. This happens occasionally in personnel interviews and is known as the "halo effect." The interviewee who thus hooks the interviewer can then do no wrong in the eyes of the interviewer. The interviewer's placing of personal positive qualities onto the interviewee may override strong evidence to the contrary.

These illustrations demonstrate undesirable situations but they nevertheless demonstrate the power of positive projection. Therefore we do well to realize the presence of potential positive dimensions of our shadow a well as negative. We need to list these qualities we admire and deeply admire in other people. Then when we hear ourselves saying, "Oh, but I could never be like that," we would do well to investigate those traits, for they are undoubtedly a part of our Golden Shadow.

EXAMINING OUR "SLIPS"

A third pathway into the personal shadow is to examine our slips of tongue, slips of behavior, and misperceived behaviors. Slips of tongue are those unintentional misstatements that cause us no end of embarrassment. When we say that among other things shadow is all that we would perhaps *like* to be, but wouldn't dare, we set the stage for shadow's appearance through these phenomena. "That is absolutely the last thing I wanted to say," or "I can't believe I said a thing like that," and similar "apologies" demonstrate that while consciousness proposes, shadow often disposes.

For example, Ann had been taught always to put the most charitable construction on all that others do. Therefore, when her friend Chris decided at age sixty to enter modeling school, Ann wanted to commend her, even though she privately thought it rather ludicrous. Her shadow told her just *how* ludicrous when Ann, wishing to be congratulatory of Chris's decision, told her: "I'm sure you will be an *outstanding* muddle." Of course she meant to say "model," but she was unaware of just how critical she was of Chris's decision. Instead, she said (or shadow said) "muddle," which was what Ann truly assessed the situation to be.

Slips of behavior are perhaps even more revealing. Sometimes there seems to be absolutely no explanation for a person's "aberrant" behavior. Someone will say, "I don't know what got into him; I've never seen him act this way!" The behavior seems totally alien to the generally perceived nature and disposition of the person and all (including the person) are dumbfounded by the experience.

Charles was known by his colleagues to be a gentle, charitable and caring person. In his office he often played the role of conciliator whenever differences arose and disputes occurred regarding who was "right." One day Charles and two colleagues went to lunch at a quiet restaurant. Charles drove, and parked in the small lot behind the restaurant.

After a pleasant and friendly lunch, the three got into Charles's car to drive back to work. Charles backed the car into the narrow alleyway behind the restaurant and slowly proceeded toward the intersection with the next street. Just then a car pulled into the alleyway from the street and slowly headed toward Charles. The alleyway was much too narrow for two cars to pass, so one or the other would have to back up. Neither car, however, stopped until they were facing each other bumper to bumper. Charles began to gesture wildly for the other driver to back up and get out of his way. He began to shout at the driver and curse him. Then he sat, clutching the wheel, staring fiercely ahead. He said to his companions, "You can walk back to the office if you want, but I'm not going to budge from this spot till that _____ moves, even if it takes all afternoon." The driver of the other car finally capitulated and backed up to the intersection, with Charles pursuing him only inches away.

Driving back to the office, Charles was his "normal" self, seemingly having totally discounted the incident. One of his colleagues asked, "What the heck was *that* all about?"

"What?" responded Charles, innocently.

"That tug of war back there."

Suddenly Charles flushed and sputtered and became effusive with apologies and explanations, and then again returned to his usual demeanor. The two colleagues looked at each other, and simply shook their heads, mystified.

Still another type of "slip" occurs when one is perceived other than as one intended to be perceived. For example, a speaker may intend to present herself quite congenially to her audience, only to be informed after her presentation that she "came across very sarcastically." A modest, shy woman may be offended by the "advances" of men at a party, being totally unaware of her sexually flirtatious manner. A man called on to deliver a brief speech honoring a colleague at an awards dinner was mystified when his spouse told him after the event how "nicely derogatory" he had been in his humorous remarks.

The more often we are perceived other than we intend to be perceived, the less we know ourselves and the more we would benefit from entering into ourselves through the shadow's door. The speaker, for instance, seeing her resentment behind her congeniality, has the opportunity to examine this characteristic and learn something more about her inner self. Is she unhappy doing what she is doing?

Was there something about the subject or content of her presentation that facilitated her shadow's appearance? Does she have feelings about people in the audience, or about the group itself, that are strongly opposite to her conscious awareness?

The modest and reserved woman can benefit from examining honestly her feelings and attitudes about her own sexuality as a result of this discovery of being perceived quite differently than she intended. Likewise, the man speaking at the awards dinner has the opportunity now (should he choose to take it) to look at his dark brother of jealousy, envy, and resentment.

In all such situations (which certainly are common experiences to all of us) we are given the opportunity to journey inward to discover more of our selves, and benefit from that discovery. We can choose either to do it or not. It will do us no good to laugh off such "slips," or to become defensive, or to rationalize, or to sweep them under the rug. Boldly facing them will allow us to discern the darkness in our shadow, but will also profit us with the gold of deeper understanding of ourselves, which in turn may disallow these embarrassing, awkward, even destructive "slips."

CONSIDERING OUR HUMOR AND IDENTIFICATION

A fourth pathway into the personal shadow is the examination of our humor and our response to humor in general. Most of us know that humor is often much more than meets the eye; in fact, what is said in humor is often a manifestation of shadow truth. People who strongly deny and repress shadow generally lack a sense of humor and find very few things funny.

Consider, for example, the old story of the three clergy in a small town who got together weekly in a "support group" of sorts. The longer they met the more intimate and trusting of each other they became. One day they decided that they had reached the level of trust where each could confess his gravest sin to the others and thus share his guilt. "I confess that I steal money from the offering," said the first. "That *is* bad," said the second, who then went on to confess, "My gravest sin is having an affair with a woman in the adjacent town." The third clergy, hearing the wretchedness of the other two declared, "Oh my brothers, I must confess to you that my most terrible sin is gossip; and I can't wait to get out of here!"

Most of us laugh at the conclusion of the story because it is funny, we say. But more than that, the story hooks our own shadow element of gossiping and we delight in identifying with the expected pleasures the third man will enjoy as he spreads the word around town abut the sins of his two colleagues. Of course we *know* it is wrong, and we certainly wouldn't do such a thing; but remember, among other things, shadow is all that we wouldn't dare do, but would *like* to do. Finding the story funny actually enables us to perceive ourselves a little more clearly. On the other hand, the person who denies and represses shadow will find no humor in it, but will instead be judgmental of it all. Such a person will conclude that the story is not funny, but sad—it is yet another indictment of our times, they would say, and all three clergy should be punished.

We *know* that it is very bad taste to delight in another's pain or misfortune, and yet we find the antics of a person on ice skates for the first time to be exceedingly funny. Decades ago, one of the first scenes to delight viewers of the new "moving pictures" was the classic fall as a result of slipping on a banana skin. We howl at the exasperated comic who tells of the many misfortunes under which he or she suffers. The humor of these situations evokes laughter as the repressed sadism in us finds expression. Clearly, examining what we find to be humorous and especially funny will also help us to greater self-knowledge.

The factor of identification with others is somewhat related to the matter of humor. For example, we identify with the third clergy in the above story and vicariously live out our repressed shadow characteristic of gossiping.

Literature, drama, television, and movies provide countless characters with whom we may identify. Since such identifications may provide us with vicarious expressions of our forbidden shadow dimensions, it is therefore helpful to note the types of characters with whom we identify, what they symbolize, and how they behave.

Often we find ourselves admiring the "bad guys." It is not unusual for people to root for the crooks in a chase. We expect that good will prevail in the end: but in the meantime, let the criminals successfully leap the rising drawbridge in their car, and let the police get dunked in the river.

If the author of a novel has caused the antagonist to overcome, through unlawful acts, injustices that have been done, we may find ourselves saddened when the antagonist finally comes to an end and is done in. The antagonist has provided a vicarious expression of our repressed shadow, which prefers unacceptable vengeance over persona's "appropriate" forgiveness. Noting the traits and attitudes of characters with whom we identify can provide an invaluable resource for uncovering our shadow's dimension.

We may frequently observe the magnitude and intensity of shadow at a sports event, particularly a contact sport. Behavior that would probably result in fines and imprisonment in any other setting is appropriate, possibly encouraged, and even applauded in this one. Suggestions bordering on murder may be made by otherwise gentle people. I once encountered a group of elderly women while I was attending a professional wrestling match to do a sociological survey. I was so fascinated by their behavior that I forgot to do my survey. They were quite "normal," until the wrestlers stepped into the ring. But when the match began they stood up, shook their fists, and shouted, "Kill that no-good, lousy bum!" "Don't let him get away with that; break his arm!" Vicarious expression of shadow aggression was the order of the evening.

STUDYING OUR DREAMS, DAYDREAMS, AND FANTASIES

One final pathway into the personal shadow is the study or our dreams, daydreams, and fantasies. While we may wish to argue to the contrary, all of us dream, daydream, and fantasize. If we begin to pay attention to these experiences, we stand to learn a great deal about our shadow and its contents.

When shadow appears in our dreams it appears as a figure of the same sex as ourselves. In the dream we react to it in fear, dislike, or disgust, or as we would react to someone inferior to ourselves—a lesser kind of being. In the dream we often want to avoid it, frequently sensing that it is in pursuit of us, when it may or may not be . Shadow may also appear as an indistinguishable form we intuitively fear and want to escape.

Since the figure is our own shadow, or some representative part of our shadow, we need to face it and discover what it is and what it is about. We need to observe its actions, attitudes, and words (if any). Since it personifies dimensions of ourselves that could be conscious, it is a helpful resource to knowing ourselves. The usual tendency in the dream, however, is to avoid the shadow, just as it is for many of us in conscious life.

We may want to deny that we indulge ourselves in daydreams or fantasies, but the truth is that we spend more time at it than we care to realize. It is unbearable, if not impossible, for the conscious mind to be affixed on some concentrative function all its waking time. Therefore, what do we think about when there is nothing to think about? Where does our mind go; what images and fantasies invade our thoughts? Daydreams and fantasies can be so contrary to the persona we wear that they may even frighten us. We certainly do not intend to admit to others what these things are like, and many of us will not even admit them to ourselves.

But in denying their existence we miss yet another opportunity to know ourselves. For in our fantasies and daydreams we discover thoughts, plans, schemes, and dreams that we are unable to accept on a conscious level. These are often fantasies of violence, power, wealth, and sexual acting-out. There are also fantasies of gold and daydreams of enrichment, wherein we see ourselves as achievers of the impossible. Once again, the shadow stands ready to share its gold if we will but encounter it and reflect on it.

We must conclude that entry into one's shadow is a very personal thing, and will be unique to each person who does it. Each of us must pursue our own path of entering and following through. Even though there can be no generalized procedure for this journey inward through shadow, the above recommendations can be helpful.

As we considered earlier the reasons for journeying inward, we noted that there are three essential modes of gold to be found in shadow and made available for our conscious, creative use: the positive use of negative shadow qualities; the discovery of positive shadow qualities, which correspond to the negative, undesirable traits of our personality; and the uncovering of undeveloped and underdeveloped traits, characteristics, attitudes, and aptitudes within the shadow. In the next chapters we will consider specifically these dimensions of the journey inward to your Golden Shadow.

Part II

THE DISCOVERY

CHAPTER 6

Gold in the Mire

Once upon a time, an old man became lost in the forest, in the midst of a snowstorm. Fortunately, he came upon a great castle, which was quite comfortable but seemingly deserted. In it he found warmth, food, drink, bed, and new clothes. Next morning, as he was about to depart the castle, he plucked a branch of rose blooms to take to his lovely daughter at home. Suddenly, he heard a dreadful noise and saw coming toward him a beast so horrible that he was frightened half to death.

The monster was angry that the man had abused his hospitality by stealing the roses, and condemned him to death. He listened, however, as the man explained his purpose in taking the branch of roses—that he had promised to bring a rose to his daughter on his return from his journey. The Beast agreed to free him on the condition that he send back one of his daughters to die in his place. The man agreed. Of course he had no intention of sacrificing one of his daughters to the monster; but he wanted simply to see his family once more and would then himself return to the castle and his death.

Once home, he recounted his story to his family. Beauty, the daughter for whom he had taken the roses, declared that she would offer herself to the fury of the monster in her father's stead. She put aside the arguments of her family and persuaded her father to take her to the monster's castle. Once at the castle, Beauty could not help but tremble at the hideous apparition. "Have you come of your own free will?" the Beast asked. Beauty told him she had, and the Beast was pleased. As it happened, the Beast treated Beauty quite well, and she began to believe that she really had nothing to fear.

In time, the Beast became fond of Beauty and asked her to be his wife. She refused and he became quite sad. He persisted, but she continued her refusal. One day she asked to have permission to visit her

family briefly, for she missed them so. The Beast agreed, but demanded that she return lest he himself die of sorrow.

At home, Beauty enjoyed the time with her father, but was manipulated by her wicked sisters into staying longer than she had
agreed. In a dream, she saw the Beast lying nearly dead in the castle
garden. She returned immediately to find him unconscious, as she
had seen him in the dream. She completely forgot her horror and re-
vived him. As he told her of his grief and impending death, Beauty
said, "No, you shall not die; live and be my husband, for I cannot live
without you. I give you my hand and swear to be yours alone."

Suddenly the castle sparkled with lights, and the Beast vanished.
In his stead was a handsome prince, who quickly told Beauty that she
had freed him from a spell cast on him by an evil fairly. He had been
imprisoned in the form of a Beast until a beautiful girl should consent
to marry him.

This classic fairy tale, "Beauty and the Beast," is an excellent illustration of the observation that things are not always what they appear to be. We all know this, but often tend to forget it—especially
where the shadow is concerned. "What is bad, undesirable, or evil is
bad, undesirable, or evil," we say, "and that is that!" But "that may
not be that," as mythology and fairy tales remind us most
profoundly.

Mythology and fairy tales form the province of fantasy, but because of their timelessness and universality they are rich in symbolism of the real world. In myth and fairy tales, inanimate objects often
become quite animated; dumb animals frequently engage in rational
conversation with each other and with human beings; elements such
as air, fire, and water behave in ways totally contrary to their nature;
witlessness is not stupid, but actually wise; and beasts and monsters
turn out actually to be princes and princesses. Frequently, what appears to be evil is good in disguise.

This latter theme appears quite frequently. It generally follows a
common pattern in which a person (male or female) comes upon a
highly undesirable being (beast, monster, or hideous creature), often
well off the beaten path, not infrequently in the depths of the forest.
After a fascinating series of adventures, the person demonstrates sincere caring, acceptance, and love for the undesirable being; where-
upon it is suddenly transformed into a very desirable being—a beautiful prince or princess. The prince or princess had been transformed

into the undesirable being by a wicked entity, and only the true acceptance and love of a human being could break the spell and restore
the person to normalcy.

A story similar to "Beauty and the Beast," but possibly less well
known, is the Korean fairy tale "Tiger Woman." According to this
story, Nim San, a widower with several children, became disoriented
while climbing in the mountains near his home. Snow began to fall
and he became quite cold. He was suddenly encountered by a
uniquely beautiful woman riding in a sedan chair borne by four run-
ners. He had never seen so beautiful a face—tinted ivory skin, red
lips, delicately pointed chin, black hair, thin black eyebrows, and narrow slanted green eyes, like those of a cat. The woman invited him to
come with her to her house in a hidden valley for food, warmth, and
rest, so he might be refreshed to journey back to his home next
morning.

Her house was actually a large and beautiful palace and Nim San
was treated royally. The beautiful woman, who was quite wealthy,
sought Nim San's friendship, promising to give him all that he
should desire if he would visit her on winter evenings to play chess
and while away the hours. Nim San was delighted with the arrange-
ments and made several visits to the palace through the winter, becoming more enamored with the beautiful woman each time.

One day in early spring, while on his way to the hidden valley, a
cloud of fog suddenly descended on Nim San and the voice of an ancestor informed him that the beautiful woman was actually a tiger,
permitted only for certain hours to take on the form of a human. Nim
San was devastated; her being other than she seemed cut him deeply,
for he had come to love her. The voice of the ancestor told Nim San to
go to her palace and thrust open the door to the inner court and he
would see her in her terrible state. Furthermore, the voice told him, if
he could catch her in the act of changing into a human, she would
forever remain a fierce and hated beast, unable to deceive any more.

Nim San hurried to the palace, rushed to the inner court, and then
stopped. He could not do it. He could not take advantage of the tiger/
woman, even if by some magic art she were able to appear human
and deceive him. She had been too kind, and he loved "her."

Suddenly, the woman stood before him more beautiful than ever.
"You have saved me from a thousand years of grief and torment," she
said. "In the spirit world I was condemned to take the form of a tiger

for many generations. If, during my time as a woman, I could win the love of a good man who would marry me in spite of knowing my other state, then I could remain human. That voice you heard in the fog was not the voice of your ancestor, but of an evil spirit."

"I would rather have you as my wife," said Nim San, "whatever shape or form you held in some past life, than any woman in this world or any other."

In "Beauty and the Beast," there is a very clear message that the Beast was not at all what he appeared to be, but was something quite other, namely, a prince. Only the willingness of Beauty to overcome the undesirability of the Beast and accept him as he was could free him to be the handsome and loving human being he truly was. Having accepted that which was unacceptable, Beauty discovered in it that which was highly desirable.

The Korean tale is somewhat more complex and possibly more profound. There appears to be a double case of things not being what they appear to be. Nim San was devastated when he learned that he had been deceived by a tiger posing as a beautiful and kind woman. For a moment he may have felt powerful resentment if not disbelief, and was moved to reject and deny the beast and keep her forever in her beastly body. Nevertheless, he chose not to do that, but to accept her as she was and love her in spite of her deceit. As in the case of Beauty, Nim San's loving acceptance broke the power of the curse and freed the tiger/woman to be the beautiful and kind human being she truly was. Like Beauty, in his acceptance of that which was unacceptable, Nim San discovered that which was highly desirable.

GOOD POTENTIAL IN EVIL OPPOSITES

These fairy tales promise the very real possibility of discovering gold in even the mire of our shadow. But we still have to journey into that dark and foreboding realm. Even with strong internal motivation and full knowledge that the benefits will be profoundly rewarding, we are still strongly reluctant to walk the path into the depth of our being. We know that our first encounter is with the very darkness of our selves, and who knows what horrors we might encounter? If we abide by our premise that the human being is a creation capable of great evil as well as great good, we cannot avoid the possibility of such an experience.

Nevertheless, the good news is that there is a certain paradox about the journey inward that can provide no little amount of encouragement. The quotation from Hilton's *Scale of Perfection* spoke to it clearly. Jesus once stated it this way: "Unless a kernel of wheat falls to the ground and dies, it remains only a single seed. But if it dies, it produces many seeds. The man who loves his life will lose it, while the man who hates his life in this world will keep it for eternal life" (John 12:24–25 NIV).

So it is with this journey: We must come face to face with the possible worst in us in order to discover the prospects for a deeper and richer life and a greater fulfillment of self. If we continue to identify and own only the bright side of ourselves (persona), life will be progressively artificial, boring, and uncreative. Not only that, we will jeopardize our safety by making ourselves vulnerable to acting out the worst possibilities of our shadow. Frightening though it may be, it is also exciting in its possibilities; for it is truly only through this journey inward that we can even approach becoming what we *can* be.

It is quite reasonable that for most of us the encounter with shadow should be frightening. After all, we are facing the opposite of our conscious persona—that mask which has been meticulously fashioned to be the most acceptable image we could possibly make it. The "flip side" is nothing less than everything that was rejected by our subculture and society in general; everything that we don't want to be; everything that we would perhaps like to be but wouldn't dare; everything that we don't want to know about ourselves; the potential, as Hilton reminds us, to cast us down "from the honesty of man into a beast's likeness."

The realization that we could possibly get lost to despair in this process strongly emphasizes the importance of having a traveling companion. The more we have fooled ourselves into believing that we are only what we appear to be, the more awesome will be the discovery of our dark counterparts, and the more emotionally and spiritually devastating can be the image of the dark brother/sister that slowly comes into focus. We need a companion to take our arm and walk with us, give us support, pray with us, help us see the larger picture as opposed to becoming preoccupied with our latest terrible discovery.

The journey inward proceeds slowly, compassionately, piece by piece, revelation by revelation. We discover a new dimension of shadow and we struggle with that until we can finally own it and say, "Yes, that is a part of me."* Even after the first discovery, we have come a comparatively long way in growth toward wholeness because we have brought into conscious awareness a hitherto hidden dimension. Now we can at least do something about it. We can do nothing about that which is unconscious. As long as we avoid or deny it, that element may have control over us; we are powerless to deal with it until we make it conscious.

Once we move beyond the initial encounter with a negative shadow characteristic and accept it as truly a part of us, it becomes less frightening. We recognize its significance—we do not pooh-pooh it. We certainly may not be proud of it, but we acknowledge it and keep it in consciousness where we may deal with it.

ACCEPTING THE UNACCEPTABLE

The question of whether or not there can be a redeeming dimension in a negative shadow characteristic is of utmost importance to us in our journey inward to the Golden Shadow. Is there any possibility of a positive potential in an obviously negative trait? The answer is, "Yes, most assuredly!" I do not mean that we should discount what we encounter in the shadow and say, "Oh, it's not all that bad." No, we face the reality of it and acknowledge its negativity and its negative potential. But in the midst of this we remember that there are very few absolutes, and we allow ourselves to be open to all possibilities, reminding ourselves that things may not always be what they appear to be.

"Beauty and the Beast" and "Tiger Woman" clearly point out that there very well may be something desirable in that which appears to be undesirable. When acceptance and love is shown to the undesirable it may manifest something quite desirable. This suggests that we should not take all things at face value, but look to see if perhaps there is more than meets the eye.

Whatever the trait, characteristic, attitude, or aptitude we face in

---

*We could never take the disclosure all at once; it would be absolutely overwhelming—we would be hopelessly destroyed. Sometimes people foolishly proclaim that they want to be absolutely, nakedly honest with themselves—know themselves inside out, nothing held back. This is nothing less than an invitation to insanity. We should not for one minute discount the power of shadow or downplay the possible ramifications of discovery.

the shadow, we must accept it even in its most hideous undesirability. If we befriend the beast, it may very well turn out to have something positive to offer us. Then again, it may not. But we must allow ourselves to be open to that possibility rather than immediately condemning it (and ourselves) once we have recovered from the shock of discovery. It takes courage to look into shadow in the first place; but it takes further courage to accept, as a part of our human predicament, whatever we find; and then to see if possibly there is something positive to be gained from it. Much more often than not, there is.

This means we need to abandon the notion that all vices and virtues are absolute; that there is never a shred of virtue to be found in any vice, and virtues can be only that. This is simply not the case. Jesus told us that we can learn something from the potential materialistic thief in us. At the end of his famous Dishonest Manager parable (Luke 16) he said,

The master *commended* the dishonest manager because he had acted shrewdly. For the people of this world are more shrewd in dealing with their own kind than are the people of the light. I tell you, use worldly wealth to gain friends for yourselves, so that when it is gone, you will be welcomed into eternal dwellings. (Luke 16:8–9 NIV)

Any person who possesses a fairly well developed trait of honesty has necessarily rejected dishonesty, and consequently relegated it to the shadow domain where it lives a life of its own. Jesus is simply saying here that those of us who are honest people can benefit from the potential for dishonesty within our shadow and thus become a more whole and complete person. Do not hear him tell us to identify with the crook within us, for he does not say that. He tells us to identify and then incorporate into our conscious persona only those aspects of dishonesty that will help us develop our potential on all levels. This is particularly true for those whose persona image of honesty is quite substantial and who correspondingly are naive and trusting, assuming that all others are as they. Such "people of the light" can learn much from "people of the world" and become much less likely to be duped, taken advantage of, or cheated.

I once knew a man who had inherited considerable wealth. He was an honest and generous person who believed in the basic trustworthiness of humankind. A friend approached him one day with the proposition of joining him in partnership in a housing development project that truly promised a healthy return with little risk. If he put up the money, this friend would do all the work of development. He knew this friend to be experienced and successful in such ventures—furthermore, he was the son of a minister. So he joined the partnership with an investment of half a million dollars. He paid no attention to the progress of the project, but left it in the hands of the friend, whom he trusted. Shortly after the land purchase and the sale of a few of the lots, however, the friend absconded with all the money and was never seen again. The man was left with the loss of his investment, plus the many bills that had been incurred.

To have protected himself from such a swindle, it would not have been necessary for this man to have become any less honest than he was. It would not have been necessary for him to have become dishonest. In the parable, Jesus never suggested that honest people should become crooks themselves. Had this man, however, been more accepting of and thus in touch with his own potential for dishonesty, he would have been wiser, less blatantly trusting, and consequently less vulnerable to being abused by the cunning of his fellow human being. Had he not denied his shadow trait of dishonesty and crookedness (which would have been substantial, given the magnitude of honesty and trust in his persona), but had rather accepted it and embraced it, this apparently undesirable "beast" could have presented him with the gifts of wariness, skepticism, cunning, and "looking out for one's own neck." In this case the gold, hidden in the mire of shadow, could have saved the gold that was stolen from his pocket.

Shadow has a life of its own and clamors for attention and time on the stage. Instead of elbowing it back into the wings, and trying to continue to persuade the "audience" that we *are* only what they see, we need to turn around, face, and dialogue with shadow, undesirable as that may be, and gain reflective insight from the encounter.

THE DESIRABLE IN THE UNDESIRABLE

Through the vehicle of meditation we can accept the negative dimensions of shadow as we discover, face, and reflect on them. We meditate on that dark, undesirable aspect, looking for any facets within it that may be employed consciously in a creative, constructive way. We look for facets that may be used to balance persona's overemphasis on the opposite characteristic. For example, a meek person may discover a shadow trait of aggressive forcefulness. Through meditation, that person may accept this undesirable potential and realize that within the blatancy of aggressive forcefulness is hidden the quality of assertiveness, which can balance the person's trait of meekness and provide a richer experience of self-esteem.

Envy and covetousness are common shadow counterparts to a persona's exaggerated respect of other people and celebration of their achievements. It would be extremely upsetting to be faced with the realization that our shadow includes these demons, particularly when we have endeavored always to look up to others and applaud their achievements. To accept and embrace envy and covetousness within ourselves would be loathsome; but such acceptance could allow these shadow attitudes to provide us with the positive dimension of motivation—motivation to achieve goals, and to develop ourselves into being what we can be.

In *An Introduction to the Psychology of Fairy Tales,* psychologist Marie-Louise von Franz reminds us that

envy is a misunderstood compulsion to achieve something within oneself that one has neglected. It springs from a vague awareness of a deficiency in one's character, a deficiency that needs to be realized; it points to a lack which can be filled. The object of envy embodies what one might oneself have created or achieved.

Likewise, we may discover harsh anger that has been repressed into shadow by years of living out a sweet and godly persona. Accepting the reality of that repugnant shadow characteristic could allow us to meditate on it. We could then visualize using an *appropriate* expression of anger in confronting an intolerable situation. This could possibly free us from much physical, emotional, and spiritual stress.

Facing the blackness of greed and avarice in shadow is a terrible experience. But if we can accept and embrace it as truly a part of self, we may very well use positively the dimensions of these undesirable attributes of greed and avarice that will foster ambition and the pursuit of a goal.

I once counseled with a woman who had become separated and cut off from her sexual and erotic self. A truly feelingless marriage relationship had encouraged the repression of this dimension into shadow. Now divorced for some time, she was distressed by her inability to relate comfortably and satisfyingly to desirable men. One night she dreamed that a woman whom she identified as a "painted whore" seemed to be pursuing her. The figure in the dream was disgusting to her and she wanted to avoid her.

The woman knew she had been visited by her own shadow characteristic in the dream and was willing, however repulsive, to accept and embrace her. The "painted whore" ultimately helped restore her sexuality, helped her to be comfortable with it, and allowed her to reenter satisfying interpersonal relationships with men.

A man on his journey inward became quite distressed when he began to realize how readily he identified with fictional characters who were arrogant, haughty, and insolent. He was shocked to become aware that he delighted so in their behaviors and their deeds. In daily life he was an extremely passive man who was quite willing to place himself last, behind, or below everyone else, and put down himself and his accomplishments. Now he faced this terrible opposite in his shadow and it horrified him. He wanted to have nothing to do with it. He longed to deny it; but once he had brought it into consciousness he was compelled to find a way to live with it. Through meditation he visualized using creatively the self-acceptance that seemed to him to be present in the arrogance and insolence of shadow. Slowly, very slowly, he modified his image of himself and began to allow himself the experience of self-love.

Refusing to accept shadow elements and continuing to deny their presence in ourselves makes us less than whole persons. Trying to appear to be "better" than we are prevents our becoming what we can be.

There is virtually no end to the possibility of finding gold in the mire of shadow. Once we are able to bear the wretchedness of the reality of the trait and own it truly as our own, we invariably find that it can indeed offer up a redeeming dimension we can incorporate in our conscious self and employ to our advantage.

Nevertheless, it is of utmost importance that we do not totally identify with any of these negative, even evil dimensions that come into our awareness. To identify with shadow and act it out is dangerous and potentially destructive. Such behavior is completely different from our discussion of suffering a shadow insight (denying the temptation to act it out once it becomes conscious). We live with the tension between the old personality dimension and its newly discovered opposite until the new element is integrated into our conscious personality. We must bear the distress of owning this dark element until we find the way to incorporate it into our conscious self by using it in a creative and positive way. Through visualization in our meditation we can "see" how this integration can occur. We can facilitate this integration by visualizing ourselves as having already made the integration, and then consciously behaving as we have seen ourselves in our meditation.

Our goal on our journey is not to become the opposite of what we were. Our task is to reconcile the opposites we discover—to somehow bring the persona trait and its opposite shadow trait together into a new entity, so the white of persona and the black of shadow come together in gray. We do not move from white to becoming black, or from black to becoming white, but to a shade of gray. We endeavor to stretch out our awareness and transcend the "good" of persona and the "evil" of shadow and bring forth an entity that is neither one nor the other, but the child of both.

Such integration requires time; it is not an overnight occurrence. It requires patience with ourselves as we struggle to find the integrated level. It requires stamina and endurance to persevere in the process. Thus our flesh-and-blood traveling companion becomes a great resource of encouragement, and our faith in the power of the Spirit of God within us is a great source of strength and support.

CHAPTER 7

Scoundrels and Saints

Most, if not all of us, are quite ready to admit to the fact that "no one is perfect." This is particularly true when we are caught in a short-coming and are clearly guilty of a fault. This confession may "get us off the hook," so to speak, but it also clearly identifies that each of us develops negative, undesirable traits in our conscious persona along-side the many positive characteristics that are there.

This may not be a particularly desirable observation but it is help-ful for us to remember what the law of opposites tells us: For every trait developed in the persona, there is an equal and opposite trait residing in the shadow. So we can discover another source of gold in our shadow—truly positive shadow characteristics that are the oppo-sites of negative persona traits.

Betty is well aware of the undesirable characteristic of short tem-per in her persona. Most of the people who encounter Betty are aware of it too. If Betty should ever desire to do so, she could journey into her shadow to discover the opposite and positive trait of patience and long-suffering. Tim, whom we met early in the book, had developed a strong negative characteristic of self-effacement in his conscious persona. His journey into his shadow allowed him to discover and bring to consciousness its positive opposite of self-respect.

The motivation for us to develop the "ideal" personality is great; but it is never quite enough to enable us to fulfill entirely what is expected of us. Each of us has many undesirable characteristics in our persona; and likewise, for each shortcoming, fault, bad habit, and "missing of the mark," there is an equal and opposite positive trait (golden characteristic) in our shadow.

Furthermore, the development of a "positive" persona and a "negative" shadow is always relative to the expectations of the sub-culture in which one develops. This is to assume that those expectations are similar to the expectations of society in general. Most of the time this is a safe assumption; however, it may not be true in some cases, and in many cases it may not be true to some degree. Sometimes the standards of the subculture are far removed from or even contrary to the expectations of society in general. In such cases, the persona would be filled with what we would normally identify as negative qualities, while the shadow, comprised of the persona's opposites, would be a veritable gold mine of positive traits.

In some subcultures, the debasement of women is still a standard; consequently that would appear as a positive trait in the personas of men of that subculture, even though to society in general it would be a negative trait. Children who grow up in the atmosphere of the antisocial and criminal element develop traits and characteristics in their conscious personas that are encouraged and rewarded by that element, but regarded as negative by society in general. In cases such as these, as far as most of us are concerned, the law of opposites declares that such people have many positive characteristics (according to the standards of society in general) hidden in their shadows.

It is also evident that some people simply disregard the expectations of their subculture and society in general, whatever they are, and live out their evil tendencies as they will. They fly in the face of propriety and have little regard for others. These people are often a menace to society. Nevertheless, the law of opposites holds true here as elsewhere: the darker the persona, the greater the golden potential of shadow.

GREAT TRANSFORMATIONS

An East Indian fable speaks specifically to this latter observation. It bears the interesting title, "The Tyrant Who Became a Just Ruler":

Once there was a king who was so cruel and unjust toward his subjects that he was called the Tyrant. He was so heartless and inhumane that his people prayed night and day that they might have a new king. One day, much to their surprise, the king called his people together. He said to them, "My dear subjects, the days of my tyranny are ended. From now on you shall live in peace and happiness, for I have decide to try to rule henceforth justly and well." The king kept his word very well, and was soon known throughout the land as the Just King.

By and by one of his favorites came to the king and said, "Your

Majesty, I beg of you to tell me how it was that you had this change of heart toward your people."

The king replied, "As I was galloping through my forests one afternoon, I caught sight of a hound chasing a fox. The fox escaped into his hole, but not until he had been bitten by the dog so badly that he would be lame for life. The hound, returning home, met a man who threw a stone at him, which broke his leg. The man had not gone far when a horse kicked him and broke his leg. And the horse, starting to run, fell into a hole and broke his leg.

"Here, I came to my senses, and resolved to change my way of ruling. 'For surely,' I said to myself, 'he who doeth evil will sooner or later be overtaken by evil.' "

A chain of events in the forest provided the unrighteous king with a revelation that "brought him to his senses." The revelation seems simple, but to the king it was profound. We hear the king's response to the subject's inquiry and we are amazed! Humankind has known this basic tenet for centuries. Surely this was no new insight to such a worldly man. Why now?

Whatever the reason (and, of course, no one will ever know what it was), at that point in the king's life—at that very moment—everything fell into place, and he was ripe to perceive that his evil practices would eventually be his downfall. He heard a voice from within. Quite possibly he had heard it many times before, but this time he listened to it. He vowed to turn his life around 180 degrees, and he succeeded in doing it. The evil persona was overcome by the Golden Shadow.

The fable is reminiscent of Jesus' encounter with a man named Zacchaeus (Luke 19: 1–10). This wealthy man, quite small of stature, was the chief tax collector for the region of Jericho. He was charged by the Roman government to collect a certain amount of revenue from the people of the area. His salary was any amount he could collect above that quota. Tax collectors were notorious for charging their people exorbitant sums and pocketing the extra money, and Zacchaeus was no exception. Their extortion was possible because they had the power of the Roman government to back them up and protect them. Thus people paid Zacchaeus the tax he assessed them, but they despised him and treated him like an outcast.

As Jesus entered Jericho one day, people lined the road to see him. Zacchaeus was so short that he had to climb a tree to get a glimpse of him. As Jesus approached him he stopped, told Zacchaeus to come down, and invited himself to the tax collector's house for the day. Everyone was amazed (not the least Zacchaeus himself) that Jesus would go into the house of this thieving traitor. Once inside, Zacchaeus stood up and said to Jesus, "Look, Lord! Here and now I give half of my possessions to the poor, and if I have cheated anybody out of anything, I will pay back four times the amount."

When we understand the principle of opposites, it is not difficult to see the extravagant philanthropist emerge out of the shadow of Zacchaeus. The magnitude of his thievery (persona) was matched by the magnitude of his generosity (shadow). He quite literally proved the doctrine that the human being is a creature capable of great good as well as great evil.

A most profound illustration of this phenomenon is cited by Viktor Frankl in *Man's Search for Meaning*. Frankl, an Austrian psychiatrist and founder of logotherapy, survived three grim years at Auschwitz and other Nazi prisons during World War II. In his book he refers to a certain Dr. J., whom he calls "the mass murderer of Steinhof—a Mephistophelean being, a satanic figure."

When the Nazis began their euthanasia program at Steinhof (the large mental hospital in Vienna), Dr. J. was put in charge. He was so fanatic in his task that he tried not to let even one psychotic person escape the gas chamber. When the war ended and Frankl returned to Vienna, he inquired about Dr. J. and was told that he had been imprisoned by the Russians in one of Steinhof's isolation cells. Dr. J., however, somehow disappeared, and was not seen again. Frankl concluded that Dr. J., like many of his comrades, had made his escape to South America.

Some years later, Frankl had as a patient a former Austrian diplomat who had himself been imprisoned many years behind the Iron Curtain in Siberia and in the Lubianka prison in Moscow. Quite unexpectedly, the man asked Frankl if he had ever known Dr. J., Frankl said he had, and the man told him that he had met Dr. J. in Lubianka. Dr. J. had died at about age forty, from cancer. "But before he died," the man told Frankl, "he showed himself to be the best comrade you can imagine! He gave consolation to everybody. He lived up to the highest conceivable moral standard. He was the best friend I ever met during my long years in prison!"

Since about 1972, the Delancey Street Foundation of San Francisco has provided a residential treatment center for former drug abusers, prostitutes, and convicts. Most people who enter Delancey Street have hit bottom, having been convicted of various crimes, mostly violent. They have served, on the average, four terms each in prison. They enter Delancey Street bitter, angry, and cynical, displaying a vicious hatred of society.

Mimi Silbert, who has been the leader of Delancey Street almost since its beginning, identifies the teaching of belief and love as the foundation blocks of the program. Learning this takes tremendous courage by the residents because they are so afraid. It is risky to care, be close, and trust; it is extremely difficult for people who have been hurt and have hurt others all their lives. It takes a long time for them to make their leap of faith—to declare, "I can be decent."

Nevertheless, more than five thousand people have graduated from Delancey Street since its beginning. Many of them are now attorneys, police officers, teachers, and corporate executives. They present themselves as witnesses to the power of the Golden Shadow.

As we approach considering how we might discover the desirable shadow opposites of undesirable persona traits, it is perhaps helpful and encouraging to recount stories such as those above to remind ourselves of the great transformations that can and do take place. We are never so naive as to believe that such transformations occur overnight. Sometimes they do, but by and large, these experiences are processes wherein the emerging Golden Shadow is nourished and integrated into conscious behavior. Time and nourishment are the key ingredients.

REVERSAL OF VALUES

We have observed that "negative" personas may develop because people fly in the face of propriety and disregard the expectations of the subculture and society in general. It is likewise true that heavily negative personas develop because the subculture's expectations are contrary to those of society in general. As one seeks to be accepted under one's subculture's standard, the resultant conscious personality is largely in opposition to the expectations of society in general. A young man named Ed clearly demonstrated this situation.

My first encounter with Ed was during his admission to the adolescent psychiatry unit. He was enraged, swinging his arms and shouting curses to everyone and to no one. He wanted no part of being where he was, but agreed to enter the "time-out" room until he had quieted down and had worked out his feelings.

The next day a colleague told me that Ed had been verbally abusive of staff on the unit later that previous evening, claiming that we were all a bunch of hypocrites and, as usual, no one cared about him. When someone suggested that he elaborate a bit on that he said, "You tell me you care about me, but you don't. I've been here six hours now and nobody's hit me yet."

As it turned out, this was only one of many value reversals that Ed had experienced, but it was a very significant one. For most of us, and for society in general, caring is expressed through demonstrations of kindness and affection; hitting someone is a sign of rejection and a desire to hurt the person. In Ed's value system the precise opposite was true. Consequently, his interpretation of our behavior was, for him, accurate.

As time went on, I learned other dimensions of Ed's standards. Affection was best shown by a hard punch on the arm or thigh, or by knocking out of your hand whatever you might be carrying. Acceptance in the subculture was to break into and rob an automobile without getting caught. Stealing of any kind was highly valued. Belligerent behavior was the norm.

In the environment of the unit, Ed continually bumped into values that were much more respectful of self and others. On the one hand, this caused him distress and he became angry; on the other, it helped him recall values once known but long buried or abandoned. One day in a moment of insight he said to me, "I don't know how I got so screwed up. It just gets that way, I guess. Getting into trouble is no big deal; it's sort of like what you do. After a while it's just natural to act out."

Ed was on the treatment unit for many weeks. In time, caring through the kindness of words and acts of concern emerged from his shadow to replace persona's old standard of "caring" by hitting. In many of our conversations together we talked about his belligerent behavior, and how a gentle man was there in his unconscious ready to emerge.

Regression, as always, was part of the process. On Halloween, the residents and some staff from the unit dressed in costume and toured the hospital. Ed had told me that he would like to dress as a priest, and asked to borrow a clergy shirt and collar. He had the idea to carry a crucifer cross with him; so, in occupational therapy, together we fastened a wooden cross onto the end of a long pole. When the group on its tour got into the cafeteria, Ed went from table to table "blessing" the diners. "Peace on you, and peace on you," he would say; only the way he pronounced it sounded more like the performance of a bodily function than a wish for tranquility.

When Ed was discharged from the unit he moved into a group home. His transformation into a responsible young man had begun. I did not see him again until one day I ran into him outside the air terminal, in the parking area. He was working for a major car rental firm, responsible for the dispatch and return of the automobiles. We spoke briefly, and I left him, confident of his ongoing transformation.

It is important to note that in all the above accounts, the essence of each transformation came from *within the person*. Sometimes we do not know why the emergence of positive shadow elements occurs or why it occurs at the time it does. But one thing is clear: This phenomenon comes from within, because it is shadow material become conscious, and shadow is definitely a part of ourselves.

Sometimes people mistakenly believe that external forces or situations *create* these transformations. Consequently, pious humanitarians sometimes believe that "goodness" can somehow be funneled into "bad people" and they will be converted or transformed. External dimensions can encourage, nourish, and support the emergence of a positive shadow opposite; and they can provide a positive environment in which this can occur. People become recivilized, reeducated, and resophisticated. But the material for change can come only from within the person.

When, for example, Jesus visited Zacchaeus in his house he did not somehow infuse into him a deep concern for people or imbue him with a fantastic compulsion for philanthropy. He had seen in Zacchaeus an interest that went beyond mere pedestrian curiosity about the new teacher, and possibly even a preconscious desire in the little man to let down the inner bars to an extravagant generosity. Jesus demonstrated his acceptance of an otherwise unacceptable man, and provided him with an atmosphere wherein transformation could take place—wherein the bars could be let down and shadow could come crashing through into consciousness.

VISUALIZING THE OPPOSITE

No doubt it is true that we want to be blind to our obvious faults and the undesirable dimension of our disposition. Yet we can acknowledge, at least to ourselves, that our personas *are* pocked with traits and characteristics that could well be changed for the sake of a richer and more complete experience of life. We have only to look into our daily round of personal interactions and we are quickly reminded of these maverick traits. They rise up again whenever we pause to take inventory of ourselves, and we somewhat sincerely declare that we really ought to do something about them.

People usually think in terms of "overcoming" these things, such as, "I really ought to try to overcome my impatience," or "I should try to overcome my short temper." Instead of concentrating on overcoming, we need to focus our energies on visualizing the emergence of the opposite of these traits from our hidden shadow. Focusing on overcoming is often self-defeating. It is like repeating to yourself, "I will not think of the number eighteen." You end up thinking of nothing but the number eighteen.

A very helpful method for encouraging the emergence of positive shadow traits to reconcile with their opposite negative persona characteristics is the use of visualization within meditation. In this process, we actually "see" (visualize) what it is that we expect to happen. We use the positive power of imagination. Most of us know the negative power of imagination, for we even have phrases in our language that speak to it: "I just let my imagination run away with me," and "I imagined the worst." Fear becomes the product of negative imagination and we end up in the trap of a self-fulfilled prophecy saying, "See? I knew it was going to happen."

When we use visualization and positive imagination during meditation, we can employ the same power toward a positive expectation. Instead of expecting the worst, we can expect to happen what we want to have happen. Since meditation is essentially a spiritual exercise, our imagining or visualizing is actually an act of faith in which we employ the power of God within us. In many rituals and liturgical rites of the church and of religious (and even some secular) organizations, the person who is a candidate for a position or to fulfill a certain function is asked, "Will you do this?" or "Will you do that?" The person's reply is, "I will, with the help of God." We do not assume that we can accomplish our goal through the exercise of human willpower alone. Through our faith and our belief in the powers of God, which are truly a part of our very being, we incorporate the strength of spirit and will both in our meditation and in the actual living out of our visualizations.

The imaging in meditation is in a sense a "dress rehearsal" for the real-life situations for which we are preparing. The more vivid we can make the images, the better prepared we will be for the actual acting out. Suppose that we choose to deal with our undesirable characteristic of impatience. The impatience is not so great that it becomes the grounds for alienating people or severely disrupting relationships, but it *is* disturbing and simply compounds the natural annoyances of life.

We assume the meditative attitude and posture described in chapter 4. We relax our bodies and focus on our breathing, inhaling and exhaling deeply. In our mind's eye, we picture ourselves in a concrete situation where impatience has been known to occupy us. Suppose the scene is in our automobile, in "slow-and-go" traffic. The delay is aggravating and impatience is taking over. We recreate the scene as we have experienced it so many times, and see ourselves in our impatience and fuming as vividly as possible.

Next we imagine the opposite of this attitude, which we know is in existence in our shadow, and enflesh what that would look like and feel like. We visualize patience. It is helpful to "see" various nuances of the word itself—indulgence, forbearance, endurance, forgiveness, inexcitability, leniency, perseverance, tolerance, and resignation. We see ourselves quietly resigned to that which we truly cannot control. We see ourselves reaching and turning on the radio to tune in relaxing music, or putting a tape of relaxing music into the tape deck. We see ourselves breathing deeply in and out, relaxing our bodies and reversing the build-up of tension. In all, we create as vivid a scenario as we can, and firmly believe that we will be able to experience it in actuality the next time we are in this situation in real life.

We may repeat the exercise, visualizing other situations that make us impatient and imagine how our shadow opposite of patience would appear if we were to let it break through in those experiences. Possibly it is the experience of waiting in a line, or being put on "hold" on the telephone, or teaching someone how to do a task. Because we know the potential opposite of each undesirable facet of personality is resident within us, we can be all the more confident that our positive expectation will materialize. If grouchiness and dissatisfaction is a conscious characteristic, we can visualize shadow's opposite of contentment. Shadow's even temper can come forward to balance a short temper in personality.

Thus another source of gold in shadow manifests itself in the form of a tremendous array of positive elements that exist as equal opposites to the undesirable dimensions we possess in our conscious personality.

CHAPTER 8

The Undeveloped Self

Remember Tim, the man whom we met in chapter 1? He is a marvelous example of a person who discovered a long-buried potential within himself, and went on to fulfill his discovery. His strong wish to be somehow involved with computers, which slipped through the cracks of consciousness early in his life and lodged itself in his shadow, was brought back into consciousness during his journey inward, and lived out to his joy and satisfaction.

Tim is illustrative of many people who have journeyed into the shadow of their being and emerged with the gold of an undeveloped self. Doris, for example, seemed to be a shy, introverted woman who possessed little self-esteem and self-confidence. Her journey inward revealed to her the opposite qualities of assertiveness and extraversion, and the willingness to risk a small business venture. She discovered something that she believed she knew already—that she was what we might call a home handyperson. She began a home maintenance service and became joyously fulfilled in her business providing minor repairs, wallpapering, and painting.

We have seen that there is much to be gained from bringing into consciousness those hidden, "undesirable" dimensions of ourselves and finding positive potential in them. And, we also have observed that for every dark and undesirable attribute in our personality, there is an opposite desirable characteristic in our shadow that we can bring into consciousness and employ for a richer experience of life.

But beyond these two dimensions, which are sources of true gold in the shadow, there lies that vast, untapped resource: the undeveloped self. There are many facets to the undeveloped self; we will explore several of them.

OUR OTHER ATTITUDE AND FUNCTIONS OF PERSONALITY

Earlier we looked briefly at extraversion and introversion. Jung called these the two *attitudes* of personality. Some people in the process of their development are predisposed to become *more* extraverted than introverted; others are predisposed to become *more* introverted than extraverted. Both are human potentials; no one is ever completely one or the other.

Since we cannot develop all our human potentials at the same time, we develop either extraversion or introversion, reject its opposite, and relegate it to the shadow. There it remains as an undeveloped or inferior attitude. People who are consciously extraverts possess the inferior attitude of introversion in their shadows. People who are consciously introverts possess the inferior attitude of extraversion in their shadows. We place no value qualifications on these attitudes, but rather realize that both are potentials of personality. The opposite attitude of one's conscious orientation is a substantial portion of the undeveloped self, ripe for discovery.

Jung also identified four *functions* of personality—two pairs of opposites. Again, these functions are perceived as neither good nor bad, desirable nor undesirable; and none is preferable over any other.

One pair of opposites are the two functions of perception Jung identified as *irrational* functions: sensation (or sensing) and intuition. Perception is simply the manner in which we apprehend and discern (perceive) reality. The other pair of opposites are the two functions of judging Jung identified as *rational* functions: thinking and feeling. Judging relates to our making judgments, evaluations, and decisions. The functions of perception are identified as irrational because they are prerational. We perceive first, and then we judge, evaluate, and decide. The judging functions are identified as rational because they determine *how* we make judgments, evaluations, and decisions.

Each of us is predisposed to develop one or the other of each of these pairs of opposites and posit them in our personality, while the opposite functions, which are rejected, are relegated to shadow status as inferior functions. These, then, add to the potential of the underdeveloped self along with the inferior attitude in the shadow.

If we review the characteristics of the four functions, the opposing differences within each of the two pairs become clear. Certainly sensing and intuitive types both use their bodily senses to perceive the world around them, but intuitive types perceive through intuition as well—that is, through perception of reality not yet conscious. Sensing types are attuned to facts and fine print, intuitives to hunches and that which has barely reached consciousness. Sensing types prefer using familiar, learned skills, rather than learning new skills; whereas intuitive types enjoy pursuing new skills rather than continuing to practice the old skills. Sensing types enjoy and are satisfied by that which pleases the bodily senses; intuitives by that which is imaginative and fantastic. Sensing types are comfortable with precision and thoroughness; intuitive types like illusion and symbols. Sensing types tend to details; intuitives see the big picture.

The opposites of thinking and feeling types are likewise clear. "Feeling" in this sense refers not so much to emotion, but rather to values and evaluation. Often the emotion of the feeling-type person, however, is more apparent than the thinking type. Thinking types are logical and analytical; feeling types are relational and judge in terms of values, even if they appear to be illogical. Thinking types are more interested in and attentive to ideas and things; feeling types value close and harmonious interaction with people. Thinking types do not need harmony; feeling types are distressed by conflict and argument. Thinking types are straightforward, strict, and consistent; feeling types are considerate, gentle, and evaluate each situation on its own.

Our undeveloped attitude and functions reside in our shadow selves. Like negative shadow traits, these characteristics often tap our shoulders and push for time on the stage. Unfortunately, we usually elbow them back down the cellar steps, holding fast to our "one-sidedness" and rejecting "well-roundedness." Rather than learn from those unheeded voices within ourselves, we continue to regard them as *only* inferior and therefore undesirable.

Lester is an extravert, whose introvertive attitude is hardly developed at all. He scoffs at experiences of retreat, quiet solitude, introspection, and meditation and avoids them at any cost. Lou is an introvert. His extravertive attitude is substantially underdeveloped, so he refuses action and variety, group activity, and noisy celebration, preferring to let things be as they are. Such protracted sameness often lead Lester and Lou to be bored and dissatisfied without knowing why. It can be a significant part of the experience of malaise.

The same is true of the four functions. Instead of calling up and embracing intuitive-type characteristics, sensation types deny them. Rather than entertaining sensation-type traits, intuitive types clutch intuitive-type characteristics alone. Likewise thinking and feeling types. People prefer to maintain the status quo rather than look into shadow to behold dimensions of an underdeveloped self.

Discovering and seeking to develop the characteristics of our underdeveloped attitude and functions can be stressful. The thought of being something other than we are may be enough to successfully inhibit any participation in this journey within. All this is reasonable; for to behold an opposite personality trait in shadow is for some people as upsetting as to discover the potential of criminality lurking there. People say, "I have been such and such a type of person for so long, I would be afraid to be anything else." Such a statement simply discloses the unnecessary limitations that we put on ourselves by failing and refusing to bring forth this gold from our shadow. Such reluctance, while understandable, is unfortunate, because it cheats us out of realizing the great possibilities of our potential.

It is interesting to observe the reactions of people who do "try on" the opposite attitude or functions in the process of their journey inward. Most say, "Why didn't I do this long ago? This is so much more than what I was." Bill, who was described by his psychologist friend as being "hopelessly extraverted," discovered his opposite of introversion and became enriched by the enjoyment of quiet, solitude, and, as he phrased it, "the absence of people."

Again, we do not seek to *become* our opposite; we enter shadow to discover more about our lesser attitude and our inferior functions. The purpose is a greater conscious development of these undeveloped or underdeveloped characteristics so we might achieve a fuller experience of balance within ourselves, and a greater realization of the person we can be.

Meditation and visualization, as described earlier, are quite effective in helping us to befriend the other side of our personality. Reading books that elaborate on the characteristics of the attitudes and functions of personality can help us gain a clearer picture of our undeveloped counterparts and thus facilitate our creation of vivid visualizations.*

---

*I particularly recommend the work of Isabel Briggs Myers: Isabel Briggs Myers, *Introduction to Type*, Rev. ed. (Palo Alto: Consulting Psychologists Press, 1987); Isabel Briggs Myers and Mary H. McCaulley, *Manual: A Guide to the Development and Use of the Myers-Briggs Type Indicator* (Palo Alto: Consulting Psychologists Press, 1985); Isabel Briggs Myers with Peter B. Myers, *Gifts Differing* (Palo Alto: Consulting Psychologists Press, 1985).

SHEDDING VALUES COMPROMISED BY THE SUBCULTURE

The attitude and functions that develop in our conscious personality are largely the result of our predisposition toward them by virtue of the uniqueness of our creation. As we have noted, however, development of persona is largely a matter of compromise. The influence of the subculture "conditions" the developing personality, not infrequently overwhelming it; shaping, modifying, moulding, and adjusting it often into something quite other than its natural disposition.

For example, virtually all of us are endowed at birth with the natural ability for and tendency toward the expression of feelings. Our "training," however, may take place in a subculture where the expression of feelings is either not acceptable, is highly undesirable, or is strongly discouraged. Sometimes parents strongly discourage the expression of anger in children, encouraging them rather to present themselves always as pleasant and peaceful. Such parents may hide their own expressions of anger behind closed doors, particularly in marital conflict situations, so that their children are not exposed to their double standard. They may reinforce the standard by pointing out that angry people hurt and even kill other people. They may add, furthermore, that anger is sinful and spiritually unrighteous, and that God does not like an angry person.

A person who thus develops the personality trait of pleasantness and peacefulness, denying anger its appropriate expression, necessarily relegates to shadow the power and ability to express anger appropriately. This is truly a Golden Shadow attribute, as is the power and ability to express appropriately *any* strong feeling that has had to be repressed because of the expectations of one's subculture.

Often children are strongly encouraged to deny and repress feelings of grief and loss in order to reinforce the dimensions of pleasantness and stoicism in their persona. An important value of the subculture may be to appear "strong" in the face of adversity; to "go to pieces" may be branded as weakness, lack of spiritual faith, and poor adaptability.

I once spoke with a woman in a geriatric psychiatric unit who had developed under such a subcultural value as this. Agnes had regarded highly the trait of stoicism that had held such a prominent position in her life. She had been proud to have "borne up" under the many losses she had experienced. Now, however, she was suffering

under a depression that had virtually immobilized her. Her protracted stoicism had denied her grieving the loss of her husband who had
died several years earlier. Shortly before her husband died, Agnes
had been deeply impressed by the stoicism demonstrated publicly by
the wife of a prominent public figure at the time of his death. Agnes
took this woman as a model and said to herself, "If she can do it, so
can I." Unfortunately, Agnes's stoicism appeared to be partly responsible for her depression.

A positive therapy for her was to journey inward to her shadow
and discover the golden healing power of openly grieving the loss of
her loved one. In the process of giving vent to her long repressed feelings, Agnes slowly emerged out of her depression and returned to a
more enriching experience of life than she had known in years.

It is not unusual for the dynamic energy of repressed feelings to
affect adversely one's physical, emotional, and spiritual life. Great
numbers of people needlessly suffer all sorts of miseries because they
hold to a value system that debases open, appropriate expression of
feelings.

Even the positive expression of joy, excitement, and celebration is
not infrequently denied for the sake of the subcultural value of
"keeping an even, steady keel" in one's personality. A man once told
me that if any one word could characterize his growing-up experience, it would be "somber." "We all had to be somber," he said.
"Mom and dad reminded us regularly that life is a serious business
and there is no room for frivolity or foolishness. Our lives were dull
and drab—we never knew joy and celebration. In our family, to celebrate was maybe to smile, and give a prayer of thanksgiving."

This man's journey inward introduced him to the undeveloped
potential of happy excitement in his experience of life. Without this
discovery, he would not even have been able to identify his former
state. Knowing no different, he would simply have continued on, accepting his experience as being the way life is.

Ebenezer Scrooge in Charles Dickens's *A Christmas Carol* provides
an interesting illustration of a person who had no vestige of joy or mer-
riment, but only had work and no-nonsense in his conscious personality. He was prodded into his unconscious to discover and live out his
undeveloped Golden Shadow traits of philanthropy, brotherly love,
and the expression of excitement, happiness, and great celebration.

People who grow up in an atmosphere that places high value on
the denial and repression of feelings usually develop into calm, tem-

perate, pleasant, and certainly unemotional adults. They may, however, feel somewhat bored, maybe dissatisfied, "short-changed" by life, and troubled with malaise. Much of what is normal to the experience of life had to be repressed into the shadow. Therefore such people possess true gold in their shadow in the form of the power to express appropriately the whole gamut of human feelings. The ability to express feelings is a God-given gift and can be one of the most healthy enrichments to one's experience of life.

DISCOVERING OUR OWN VALUES

It becomes clear that a major factor in our quest for a more full and complete experience of our potential self has to do with the adherence to the value system of our subculture. Since the values to which we subscribe strongly influence the personality we are, we would do well to examine and evaluate them to determine if they are, in fact, truly our own at this point.

We cannot forget that our conscious persona is largely the product of the expectations of the subculture in which we developed. We were civilized, educated, and sophisticated under standards that, in the value system of that subculture, were good and right. Things do change, however, and we do well to reconsider our values regularly. We stand to get ourselves into considerable trouble if we live as though that subculture were the subculture in which we live today. Often the experience of malaise comes out of our endeavor to live out values we once adopted, but which are no longer ours. But we do not know that they are no longer ours because we never take the time to scrutinize our value system to determine if we do in fact believe and stand for what we believe and stand for.

A necessary task on the journey inward is to do precisely this, and then to examine the areas where conflicts appear. When it is discovered that a value of the subculture once held is no longer a value in our current system, we should look directly for a fulfilling opposite in the shadow.

In *Psychological Types,* Jung reminds us:

Man is constantly inclined to forget that what was once good does not remain good eternally. He follows the old ways that once were good long after they have become bad, and only with the greatest sacrifices and untold suffering can he rid himself of this delusion and see that what was once good is now perhaps grown old and is good no longer.

We may complain loudly, and many do, that our developmental process is unfair—we are powerless in the face of the overwhelming influence of our subculture, particularly our parents. Many times adolescents and adults are quick to lay the blame for all their miseries on their parents. Many times some of these accusations are accurate. In fact, given the imperfection and sinfulness of parents (and of all humanity, for that matter), every one of us could declare that our parents were guilty of "faulty programming," and that has caused us to be who we are.

Ranting and raving may help dispense the energy of one's feelings, but the real solution to the issue is nothing more than another step in the continuing process of development. It is the responsibility of all adults capable of doing so to recivilize, reeducate, and resophisticate themselves along the way. This is what we term, "Becoming one's own person." This is the problem each of us faces as we come to adult awareness. We need regularly to reconsider values. We need to reevaluate standards. What was good and right *then* may not be good and right *now*. Furthermore, what "they" believed to be good and right (or bad and improper) may be miles away from where we stand today. Unfortunately, many of us still respect and hold in high esteem persona traits, characteristics, attitudes, and aptitudes that helped us get our needs met and our wants fulfilled then, but actually work toward our destruction now.

The matter of what we do or do not do with our feelings (which was just discussed) is significant. Another important area is the realm of motivation, achievement, and performance. At one end of the continuum are value systems that discourage creativity and devaluate achievement. Such a system degrades ambition and identifies motivation as self-centeredness and egoism. At the other end of the continuum are value systems that strongly emphasize top performance and glorify accomplishment. Such a system depreciates relaxation and disparages playfulness.

People who develop within a value system that devaluates creativity and achievement have had to leave much of themselves and their potential undeveloped. Phrases such as, "You don't want to try that; you'll only fail"; and "Doing that would only be a waste of your time. Do what you know"; and "You'll never make it doing that— you'll starve" are typical of this position. The shadows of people who develop in such an environment are probable storehouses of potential interests, aptitudes, and talents. Where there is the conscious value of "Do nothing new; keep the status quo," the shadow value will encourage experimentation and exploration.

People who develop within a value system at the end of the continuum that encourages relentless hammering away at achievement, necessarily have had to repress playfulness and the delight of "wasting time just for the fun of it." Jung wrote in *Psychology and Religion: West and East,* encouraging us to remember that "shadow contains childish or primitive qualities, which would in a way vitalize and embellish human existence." Smelling the roses or picking daisies would be an enriching value present in the shadow of a compulsively driven person and would probably be ripe for development, given a chance.

Furthermore, such a value system that encourages the relentless pursuit of achievement would also necessarily place such feverish performance strongly in the realm of the outer world. After all, in our technologically oriented, extraversion-influenced society, what future is there in being a poet, artist, philosopher, writer, or musician? The future lies in finance, robotics, energy, computers—economics and technology. This is where success lies; and success in our larger culture is always measured in terms of wealth and power. There is a great potential for discovering an undeveloped "artist," for example, in the shadow of a person who holds conscious values such as these, but who realizes that these values are truly not his or her own any more, but are the residuals of those imposed upon them earlier in their development.

People who by predisposition are introverts, but who were encouraged to capitulate to a value system that accepted only extraverts, and consequently repressed their introvertive qualities, can discover undeveloped potential that gives them a satisfying sense of having "come home." There is the possibility of considerable creativity residing in the shadow of "closet introverts."

REPROGRAMMING OUR PROGRAMS

A minister once told me, "I had no intention of becoming a minister. In fact, I never wanted to become a minister; I wanted to be a salesman. But I went to a large rally for church youth when I was a senior in high school and a speaker there got me excited about being a minister. Then a counselor at the rally was very persuasive, and really impressed on me how I should pursue it, so I couldn't just let it go.

When I got home I told my parents about it and they were ecstatic. I hadn't said I was going to do it; I was asking them what they thought about it. As far as they were concerned though, I was on my way.

"So I went for it, and all through college and seminary, I thought about being a salesman. But I became a minister, and here I am."

"Have you ever thought about becoming a salesman since then?" I asked.

"Oh yeah," he said. "But I couldn't do it."

"Why is that?"

"My parents are so proud; it would devastate them."

This is not a unique story. It is not unusual for our persona to be the fulfillment of our parents' wishes. Often, however, we are not aware of this, and we may become quite disturbed with being what we are, without really knowing why. Parents, as we have noted, are quite powerful in manipulating their children, either consciously or unconsciously, particularly into being what they want them to be.

Furthermore, it is not unusual for parents, in the process of their children's development, to encourage them, either consciously or unconsciously, to live out their own unfulfilled selves—hopes, dreams, expectations, personalities. Parents in many and varied ways encourage their children to be what they (parents) want to be, rather than encouraging their children to develop into their own unique selves. Unconscious and very subtle influence is much more effective than overt influence. Often these parents are "pushers" who herd their children into personalities that are images of their own unfulfilled selves. Thus many people, through their development, become and end up doing not what *they* wanted to become and end up doing, but what mama and daddy wanted. Parents vicariously experience fulfillment through their children, often at their children's expense.

"When I was a boy growing up, money was tight in our house," said Martin. "One day I asked my mother if she would buy me a baseball glove. She said that there really wasn't any money for that, but she'd see. A few days later she handed me a package. I tore into it excitedly and opened it to find the cheapest ball glove I had ever seen. 'How's that?' she asked. Well, when you're strapped for money, you're grateful for what you get, so I said, 'Fine, Mom. Thanks a lot.'

"My birthday was about two weeks later. My present was a huge box that felt like it weighed half a ton. I opened it and found a big, black accordion. I was dumbfounded. I didn't want an accordion. What was I going to do with an accordion? 'You get ten lessons with that,' my mother said. 'You'll be able to play real well.'

"It wasn't until years later that I realized what that was all about," said Martin. "There were only four dollars for a baseball glove because my mother didn't like sports and didn't want me to play ball. But she liked music and wanted live music around the house, so she had no trouble finding three hundred dollars to buy an accordion."

In "pushing" their children, parents are often proud of their behaviors and are even commended by others for providing their children with "advantages." They say something like, "I never had the chance to do so and so; so I'm going to see to it that you have the chance." This is all well and good if the "so and so" is what the *child* wishes to do or be. When it is not, the manipulation occurs.

These observations are not meant to be critical of parents; they are intended to be merely a reporting of what frequently occurs in the process of developing personality in one's subculture. These descriptions can serve to heighten our awareness of the great positive, untapped potential resident in our shadow, simply by virtue of the natural experience of development.

ALL THAT MIGHT HAVE BEEN AND STILL CAN BE

One final realm of consideration remains as we look into shadow to find the gold of the undeveloped self. This has to do with potential that may have quickly passed through consciousness only to slip back into the unconscious, as well as potential that has never "seen the light of day."

This realm contains traits, characteristics, attitudes, and aptitudes that became conscious, but were compassionately rejected; that is, potential that was passed by and returned to the unconscious shadow because there was no opportunity to develop it, *or* it was of low priority, or there wasn't time or money.

This realm contains potential that may have come into the persona, but was unregarded, neither accepted nor rejected, only benignly ignored. It simply sat there on the great trading counter between psyche and the outer world and collected dust, until we casually brushed it back into the shadow realm to lie there as potential for some future.

It contains potential that never saw the light of day because of internal and external influences; material that has never had access to the trading counter. It is our access to the unfathomable volume of the collective unconscious.

Most of us are able to sit back, close our eyes, and recall many examples of the first two illustrations above. The story of Marie, the hospitalized woman whom we met earlier, is illustrative of this dimension. She had wanted early in life to be a deaconess but was unable to receive the training. In the years of her retirement, she "remembered" this strong wish and happily fulfilled it by becoming a volunteer worker in the hospital.

Michael wanted very much to be a kindergarten teacher when he graduated from college in 1950. But he was unsuccessful in securing such a position, and in order to be able to work he took a job teaching math in a junior high school. He did well in that position and continued in it for almost thirty-five years, until one day on his journey inward he discovered his long-forgotten desire to teach kindergarten. He became excited by his discovery and vowed, "This time I'm going to fulfill that potential." And he did! Not by becoming a kindergarten teacher, but by writing children's stories.

The journey into the Golden Shadow introduced Jan the nurse to Jan the potential realtor, which she ultimately became. The journey inward disclosed to Carl the bus driver an unknown talent for wood carving. Carl fulfilled that hidden potential and became an accomplished artist whose wooden ducks are highly prized. At age fifty-six Irene began taking violin lessons as a result of a discovery on her journey into the Golden Shadow. "Why not?" she said. "My sister, Charlotte, is finally getting her teeth straightened, and she's fifty-three!"

No doubt we all have had hopes that could not be realized because of certain lacks that could not be filled at the time. We lacked this, or we lacked that; and consequently the hope slipped away from consciousness but remained alive in shadow. Some of us were unable to develop as much potential as we wanted all at once; there was room for only so many irons in the fire at the same time. Thus it was necessary to lay aside some ambition that still lives, however, in the recesses of shadow.

We may even have entertained real possibilities: writing poetry, being an engineer, becoming more caring of others, scientific curiosity, a passion for candy-making, playing the harmonica, being assertive. We may even have "moved" them, but they "died for lack of a second." How many passing dreams lie in the unconscious; dreams we think we have forgotten? How many fantasies had to be abandoned because of their seeming impossibility. How many "what ifs" that bear the potential of "could be"?

We gather this information together and begin to shape the images of the great quantities of golden potential in our shadow. A diary or journal that we may have kept regularly or sporadically over the years will yield considerable data that we can now interpret in the light of Golden Shadow potential. A "life review" will take time, but such a written recapitulation of our history, noting a relatively detailed chronology of our development, will jog our memories about postponed dreams, value changes, personality characteristics, and yet undeveloped potential.

We add to this all the potential from examining the possibilities of what we can be, other than what we have become because of the influence of our parents and our subculture. We include the awareness of our discoveries from reexamining our value system. And we add the wealth of potential from our inferior attitude and functions. The image of this combined array presents us, then, with the golden potential of the undeveloped self.

In these last three chapters I have tried to articulate the content of shadow's wealth of potential available to any of us willing to journey inward to discover it and bring it into consciousness. In chapter 6 we discovered the potential for the gold of desirable elements even in the undesirability and evil of shadow's counterparts to persona's light. In chapter 7 we added the gold of shadow's positive elements, which are the counterparts of the undesirable facets of our persona. Here in chapter 8 we have included the content of the undeveloped self within shadow. Now our task is to move on in our journey and determine what we shall do with our great discovery. The remaining chapters will help us determine how we shall act on our discoveries and live out the Golden Shadow for the experience of the rich fulfillment of our potential.

Part III

THE FULFILLMENT

CHAPTER 9

The Power of Self-image

An Arabian tale tells of a fellow named Bahlul who went into the town baths one night to bathe and refresh himself. In the dressing room he suddenly became frightened, for it occurred to him that if he took his clothes off, he would forget who he was. To play it safe, he tied a string around his ankle. Once into the baths, however, the string fell off. Bahlul looked around and saw another man with a string tied around his ankle, for he, too, was afraid that he would forget who he was. Bahlul looked at the man and cried, "Yammah! How can this be? If you are me, who am I?"

A similar theme is present in the nursery rhyme, "The Little Woman and the Pedlar":

> There was a little woman,
>   As I have heard tell,
> She went to market
>   Her eggs for to sell;
> She went to market
>   All on a market day,
> And she fell asleep
>   On the king's highway.
>
> There came by a pedlar,
>   His name was Stout,
> He cut her petticoats
>   All round about;
> He cut her petticoats
>   Up to her knees;
> Which made the little woman
>   To shiver and sneeze.
>
> When this little woman
>   Began to awake,

She began to shiver,
  And she began to shake;
She began to shake,
  And she began to cry,
Lawk a mercy on me,
  This is none of I!

But if this be I,
  As I do hope it be,
I have a little dog at home
  And he knows me;
If it be I,
  He'll wag his little tail,
And if it be not I
  He'll loudly bark and wail!

Home went the little woman
  All in the dark,
Up starts the little dog,
  And he began to bark;
He began to bark,
  And she began to cry,
Lawk a mercy on me,
  This is none of I!

These caricatures humorously point out one of the most profound issues that faces every human being—the matter of identity and self-image. The questions, "Who am I?" and "How do I see myself?" are deep and far-reaching. It is no overstatement to declare that the single most pervasive and influential element of human experience is self-image—how we see ourselves.

The tale and the rhyme introduce us to this matter in the persons of two silly people who depend on their clothing for their personal identity. Without the benefit of his clothes, Bahlul does not know who he is; he cannot identify himself. He needs some kind of reminder. When the reminder fails, he becomes thoroughly confused and goes into a panic. The self-image of "The Little Woman" is so flimsy that even a mere alteration of her undergarments confuses her as to who she is. Her identity seems to have been so attached to this superficial attribute (her clothing) that even her subculture (her pet dog) fails to identify her once the attribute was changed. She is now a stranger.

MISPLACED IDENTITY

These characters, Bahlul and the little woman, appear quite nonsensical; but they are probably no more than thinly disguised exaggerations of any of us whose image and identity are so misplaced. They placed it on clothes; many people place it on vocation, occupation, profession: "I am the banker," "I am the teacher," "I am the programmer," "I am the plumber." Many place it on education, or lack of it: "I am the Ph.D.," "I am the dunce," "I am the drop-out," "I am the graduate student." Many place it on looks: "I am beautiful," "I am plain," "I am handsome," "I am homely." Many place it on materialism: "I am wealthy," "I am poor." Many place it on moral behavior: "I am the righteous," "I am the sinner," "I am the devil," "I am the angel." Many place it on achievement: "I am the winner," "I am the loser," "I am the success," "I am the failure."

Albert, for example, was so identified with his position that he believed he would be personally destroyed if he "failed" at what he was doing. He was the manager of a medical clinic that had come on hard times because of personnel problems. The internal climate had become so tense that Albert was afraid that he would have to resign and seek other employment. "But what else would I do?" he asked, expressing his deep anxiety over the uncertainty of his future. "I *am* this position. I visualize myself doing 'this' or being 'that' and I say to myself, 'That is not me. That is a stranger, an alien.' I am fit to do and be only what I am."

Efforts on Albert's part to journey inward to uncover dimensions of his undeveloped self generated a discovery of many aspects of his Golden Shadow. Albert, however, would not accept these insights because he would consistently say, "No, that is not me," when a new potential would present itself to him. Only when he was willing to perceive himself on the basis of radically different criteria could he be open to using the gold his shadow offered. Until that time, not unlike the little woman of the rhyme, even a minor alteration of this image of himself evoked considerable anxiety and threatened his identity.

Albert's dilemma illustrates the highly important and significant role the concept of self-image plays in our process. Insight and awareness alone is neither curative nor automatically productive of change. Discovering our undeveloped self and becoming aware of the vast gold offered by our shadow is one thing; but it is something else again to live it out creatively and constructively, to realize our potentials, and to approach a fuller experience of what we can be.

Once we have uncovered our hidden potential, and unearthed the gold in our shadow, we still have another task: What shall we do with what we have once we have it? In the remaining chapters of this book, we will review our assets and liabilities. We will pay particular attention to managing those elements and powers that would seek to hinder us on our journey: doubt, questioning, lack of confidence, fear of failure, the reluctance to risk, the lack of self-discipline, the inertia of the status quo (a body at rest tends to remain at rest), and the voices from within and without that whisper, "You'll never make it." But even these "demons" with which we wrestle have their shadow sides, which we may use creatively and constructively.

THE MAGNITUDE OF THE POWER OF SELF-IMAGE

One of the greatest powers within us is the power of self-image or self-perception. When we speak of self-image, we go far beyond the mere reflection a mirror offers us as we gaze into it. We speak rather of the image beheld by our inner eye. Self-image is our total perception of ourselves, both conscious and unconscious. It is the highly subjective composite of the myriad observations we make of ourselves. Self-image is each person's own *complete* "I am."

Self-image is powerful and pervasive; we cannot underestimate the depth and breadth of its influence. It influences us profoundly from childhood through old age, and affects virtually every aspect of our experience of life. It is like a tinted glass or filter through which we perceive, interpret, and evaluate these multitudes of experiences. Thus it is said that people of positive self-image have a "rosy" view of life in general and perceive the glass as "half full"; whereas people of poor self-image have a "gray" or "brown" view of life in general and perceive the glass as "half empty."

Furthermore, there is hardly a psychological problem (except those of biological roots) that cannot be related to poor self-image. Likewise, there is rarely, if ever, an experience of true self-fulfillment by a person who did not enjoy a positive self-image.

As a force within us, self-image is a power for good or ill that can readily raise us to heights of healthy self-love or cast us down into the depths of despair and self-effacement. Our self-image has the power to become our guide to our "destiny." A poor self-image can lead us through a destiny in which we see ourselves invariably doomed to failure in life's many experiences. A positive self-image has the power to nurture our confidence to *expect* success, but also to accept failure.

Having a poor self-image means perceiving ourselves as worthless, unlovable, valueless, without talent, incapable, and full of doubts. Having a positive and healthy self-image means perceiving ourselves as worthwhile, lovable, valuable, gifted, capable, and confident.

For the purposes of our work, we regard self-image as probably our greatest personal power either to facilitate and enhance, or to inhibit and discourage the living out of the potential of our self, once we have brought it into consciousness. A positive, healthy self-image is the foundation of our ability and willingness to act on our insights and to exploit the potential of our Golden Shadow.

THE SPIRITUAL DIMENSION

When we examine the positive, healthy self-image, we soon find that it has its foundation in our spiritual dimension. External factors may enhance a positive self-image, but they have no power to create and found it. Without the internal, spiritual affirmation of ourselves, external elements are merely so many ornaments on a lifeless tree. The greatest wealth, the strongest power, the broadest accumulation of things, the most magnificent achievements alone cannot satisfy the basic requirement. For, fundamental to our positive perception of ourselves, is the knowledge that each of us is a unique, individual creation of God, and *therefore* a person of great worth and value.

The Judeo-Christian heritage clearly supports our intrinsic value as human beings. The Hebrew Psalmist writes, "What is man that you are mindful of him . . . ? You made him a little lower than the heavenly beings, and crowned him with glory and honor. You made him ruler over the works of your hands; you put everything under his feet" (Psalm 8:4–6 NIV).

Christianity clearly identifies the love of God for human beings in the acts of Christ's birth, death, and resurrection. Jesus said, "God so loved the world [humankind] that he gave his one and only Son, that whoever believes in him shall not perish but have eternal life. For God did not send his Son into the world to condemn the world, but to save the world through him" (John 3:16–17 NIV).

Simple logic tells us that if God perceived us as being of no or little value, he would hardly have gone to these ends of incarnation, sacrifice, and resurrection. Furthermore, God's acceptance of us human beings as we are is the second great foundation block of positive self-image. This assurance provides us with the authority to accept ourselves as we are.

In chapter 3 we dealt with self-acceptance as a basic motivator for journeying inward. We come now to see its powerful input into the development of a positive self-image. Its opposite, self-rejection, will work quite successfully to talk us out of acting on our insights and prevent us from realizing new potentials. Positive self-image, however, will provide us with the courage to act on our insights and give us support on our journey toward a greater experience of wholeness and completeness as we endeavor to reconcile opposites within ourselves, live out new dimensions of our personality, and fulfill our undeveloped self.

Self-esteem—loving ourselves—is the dimension that gives value to self-image. High self-esteem is interrelated with self-acceptance. To love ourselves is to accept ourselves in a multitude of ways. In self-love, we hold ourselves in our own arms, just as we might hold another whom we love. We are warmly and tenderly compassionate with ourselves; we let ourselves in and take ourselves in; we give recognition to ourselves; we affirm and believe in ourselves; we are patient with ourselves.

LOVING SELF AS WELL AS OTHERS

All these images—compassion, recognition, patience—are clear and reasonable in terms of accepting and loving *others*. Many of us, however, find it difficult to apply these images to ourselves. Instead of taking ourselves into our arms, as we would a loved one, we push ourselves aside. Instead of letting ourselves in and taking ourselves in, we turn ourselves away. Instead of giving recognition to ourselves, we say, "I do not know you." Instead of affirming and believing ourselves, we mistreat and disbelieve ourselves. Whereas we would deal gently with and warmly accept a loved one, we frequently deal harshly with and coldly reject ourselves.

To develop a strong, positive self-image, based on our worth and value as creations of God, we will, of necessity, have to allow these kinds of shadow values to come into consciousness and confront the old values that do not allow us to do these things to and for *ourselves*. Our culture (society in general) and many of our subcultures (various forms of religious expression) have had considerable difficulty with these kinds of precepts and have encouraged us *not* to befriend ourselves such as this.

The fear of arrogance has historically been so profound that we have been told both overtly and covertly to devaluate ourselves rather than honor and respect ourselves, and to be ashamed of ourselves rather than to celebrate and be proud of the achievements we have wrought by putting to use our God-given talents. The extreme precept has been, "The lower you perceive yourself, the more God will love you." Unfortunately, people who are ashamed of themselves can hardly love themselves; the former automatically disallows the latter. Hosts of people over scores of generations have suffered whole lifetimes of anguish and deprivation because of the plague of poor self-image.

Even the term "self-love" continues to be difficult for some people to bear because they hear it as narcissism, arrogance, idolatry, or egomania. Actually, it is precisely the opposite of all these. Nevertheless, many subcultures still teach that we ought to focus our full energy on loving God and others, and abstain from any form of self-love. Ironically, the inability or refusal to love oneself automatically prohibits loving others.

Theology and psychology agree that we must love ourselves before we can love others. The person who will not love self *cannot* love others. We may say the "correct" words and go through the "proper" motions, but what we demonstrate will be inauthentic love. The "love" given will be artificial, and unconsciously the "lover" may possibly even bear resentment toward the one being "loved."

RAMIFICATIONS OF POOR SELF-IMAGE

Healthy self-image and self-esteem is of great importance in our process of discovery. Its opposite, poor self-image and low self-esteem, can evolve into deadly enemies and saboteurs that prevent us from living out new and undeveloped traits, characteristics, attitudes, and aptitudes. These saboteurs may speak in the voice of shame, overcautiousness, doubt, uncertainty, or fear. Poor self-image leads us to say things such as: "I am not worthy to do that," or "That is too good for a person like me," or "I'm not good enough, smart enough, talented enough," or "That is out of my league," or "I could never do that," or "I would fail at that." The unconscious message underlying these articulations is, "I am a not-good person—worthless. Therefore, I should not seek to develop my potential. I do not deserve it. Besides, I could never do it. I deserve only to remain as I am."

Certainly, the power of positive self-image is great; but the strength of its opposite has to be reckoned with. Poor self-image is a demon that can quietly talk us out of any and every endeavor to act on the insights gained from our journey into shadow. It is all done in the name of prudence, caution, false humility, and good sense, so that we are seduced into uttering "appropriate" statements such as those above. "That's not me; that could never be me."

Many of us live our lives so passively that we are in a sense like a fallen leaf, tossed about by the October winds. Rather than controlling our destiny and influencing our environment to the best of our ability and capability, we passively allow the outer world to write the script, develop the dialogue, and call out the stage directions for the enactment of our lives. We live reactively, not proactively. This is the safe journey; for such a traveler never violates or even questions the expectations of subcultures and culture, and is consistently accepted as a proper part of the regiment. Such a traveler need never fear journeying into unmapped terrain or uncharted waters, which only generates anxiety and heightens the possibility of accident or shipwreck. Such a traveler can enjoy the comfort of the status quo and cheerfully avoid coming to grips with anything beneath or behind the conscious self. But as this traveler moves into the elder years of life, he or she may discover a considerable degree of disappointment in the pension benefits of such a life plan.

We noted in the introduction to this book three common complaints of adults moving into later life: (1) "I did not take enough risks"; (2) "I did not assert myself enough"; and (3) "I lacked self-discipline." Our current discussion speaks directly to the number two complaint; for the quality or attribute of assertiveness is directly related to the self-image of every person.

People with poor self-image simply cannot assert themselves. A person who perceives himself or herself as a zero cannot stand up before humanity and declare and affirm, "I am a person of worth and value. I count. All the great possibilities, as well as the potential catastrophes of life, I claim as valid territory wherein to live my life. And by the help of God, I shall live it to the fullest." One must have positive self-image, healthy self-esteem, and a belief in oneself as the "apple of God's eye" to make such a bold assertion. People who possess positive self-image trust themselves and trust God enough to pick up the reins of life and actively pursue their potential. People with a poor self-image can only be content to sit in the wagon and ride to wherever it is going.

Assertiveness can arise only out of positive self-image. Sometimes people confuse aggression with assertiveness and shy away because they believe it means being forceful, harshly confrontive, and pushy, with little or no concern for others. Quite the contrary. Aggressive behavior that fits this description is the opposite of assertiveness; it arises out of poor self-image. Sometimes people overcompensate for a poor self-image by appearing aggressive. They do not like themselves and cannot, therefore, like others. They "come on" strongly to prevent others from getting close enough to see how frightened and insecure they are, and how much they truly dislike or even hate themselves.

Assertiveness grows naturally out of security, self-respect, and self-confidence. It is authentic. It does not have to be loud; it can be firm in quietness and gentleness. It is open-armed, not defensive. As our self-image grows in positive strength, we become increasingly able to take charge of our lives.

BUILDING A POSITIVE SELF-IMAGE

Self-development requires an investment of considerable time and energy, and the development of a positive self-image and healthy self-esteem is no exception. The task of reshaping or even rebuilding an image of self that has been fashioned in one form for decades is no overnight chore. It is a matter of reprogramming possibly hundreds of programs firmly established within ourselves. It is to begin to view reality in possibly a totally different fashion than the one to which we are accustomed. It is to perceive the events of life and our responses to them through differently tinted glasses than has been our habit. Our intuitive knowledge that the result is worth the effort can provide us with an incentive to begin and endure.

Again, there is little to be gained from acting out harsh anger toward our parents, teachers and others who may have been responsible for programming into us the ingredients of a poor self-image. We may be justifiably angry, but we can truly do nothing about what is past. We did not know any better then, and we believed what we were told. Now that we do know better, we can stop behaving as though we still believe what we once believed. That was then; this is now.

One by one, we let go of and free ourselves from those many messages that tell us we're no good and will never be any different. We replace "I don't count" with "I do count." We celebrate every success in abandoning poor self-image attributes and self-defeating behavior, and build on each one as a kind or "proof" of our ability to change. We *know* we can do it.

It is always helpful to make and keep a written record of achievements and accomplishments that can serve as a reminder of the positive experiences that build self-esteem. We add to this log each positive, self-affirming experience, and we watch it grow in volume. We include our relatively insignificant achievements and accomplishments—few of us are international prize winners, great philanthropists, or outstanding performers in the arts, sciences, or sports. Collecting memories of those small achievements and reviewing them regularly serves effectively to help build self-esteem.

We set small, attainable goals in the process of building self-image so that piece by piece, one day at a time, we engage in the reconstruction of our self-image and the strengthening of our self-esteem. We accentuate the positive. We do not "catastrophize" regressions and moments of backsliding into old patterns; we accept the imperfection of our being as a natural part of our humanity, and continue on in our journey. We implore the Spirit of God within us to strengthen us and shore up our courage in the awesome task of radically changing our self-perception. We pray to God that we might be empowered to love and accept ourselves even as he loves and accepts us.

We can rely on our traveling companion, whom we enlisted to walk with us, to provide support and encouragement as we work to strengthen our self-image. The traveling companion can remind us of our goals to love ourselves and to discount old messages that regularly return to gnaw at our optimism. A book such as *How to Raise Your Self-Esteem,* by Nathaniel Branden, or my book, *You Count—You Really Do,* can be very helpful in this process. There is great value also in the reinforcement available from support groups that are growth-oriented rather than problem-oriented. We can benefit greatly from regular meditation and the vivid visualization of ourselves behaving as we now want to behave. We can daily take ourselves into our arms and love the marvelous beings we are.

CHAPTER 10

The Willingness to Risk

In 1760, William Roof and his wife, Hannah, stepped aboard a sailing vessel embarking from the shores of England. The young Hannah was several months pregnant when the ship left for America, far across the Atlantic Ocean. On December 20, 1760, somewhere on the high seas, Hannah gave birth to a tiny baby girl whom she and William named Christianna Roof. That little girl was my wife's great-great-grandmother.

In 1787, Christianna married Jesse Hall. In 1803, together with their children, they pushed westward from New Jersey and settled in the Ohio territory, where they helped found the town of Hubbard. Their adventures paralleled those of most of our early pioneers; risk was an everyday occurrence in their lives.

Christianna and Jesse homesteaded the land and raised a large family. Later in life she took up the art of midwifery and helped deliver scores of white and Indian babies in eastern Ohio and western Pennsylvania during the first half of the nineteenth century. She could still be seen, well into her eighties, riding horseback through the snowy winter countryside, fording streams and fighting winds, on her mission of helping yet another child to be born into the risky business of life.

Risk had been this woman's birthright, her occupation, and her very life. Virtually every day presented a challenge, with precious little certitude and security to counterbalance it. All this notwithstanding, Christianna's days on earth spanned a century; she died quietly in her 102nd year.

I stand by the grave of Christianna Hall in the cemetery at the Old Cornerhouse Church, and I cannot help but marvel at the courage of our ancestors and the odds they overcame. We stand back in awe and pay homage to those women and men in their great fortitude and tenacity.

Not all, however, were such courageous risk-takers. There were alarmists and doomsayers even then. While Jesse and Christianna Hall were struggling to build a "new world" in America, the noted British economist, Thomas Malthus, predicted an ominous future for the world. In 1798, he calculated that the rate of food production on earth would fall so far behind the rate of growth in population that the world would starve to death, or at least fall into global poverty and degradation. His theory came to be known as the Malthusian Iron Law. Humanity would have to depend, he declared, on moral restraint, disease, famine, war, and other disaster to prevent the inevitable.

What Malthus failed to predict, however, was the ingenuity and creativity of the risk-takers of the Industrial Revolution, who, largely through the marvels of their inventions of agricultural machinery, brought about a quantum leap in productivity.

The first half of the nineteenth century saw such a flurry of risk-taking creativity that some "alarmists" became quite weary of it. Henry Ellsworth, who was the U.S. Commissioner of Patents in 1844, lamented the volume of inventions and looked for "the arrival of that period when further improvements must end." At the turn of the century, under the administration of William McKinley, a "doomsaying" director of the U.S. Patent officer urged the president to abolish the office because "everything that can be invented has been invented."

THE INFLUENCE OF ALARMISTS

The influence of the outer world is not infrequently alarmist and doomsaying in nature. There is an inertia in culture and subculture to retain the status quo, no matter what it is. This element is relatively unsupportive of, if not often critical of nonconformity, experimentation, and risk-taking. This kind of atmosphere readily causes the repression of personal potentials that "might have been," but were instead relegated to shadow. We were simply afraid to bring them to the fore and develop them because we feared rejection by the outer world.

A striking illustration of alarmist doomsaying that depicts its far-reaching potential appeared as far back as the early pages of the Old Testament (Numbers 13 JB). The Israelites, freed from their Egyptian bondage, were led by Moses on an arduous journey through wilderness, desert, and wasteland toward the "promised land" of Canaan. Before entering, however, Moses sent out a group of twelve men to reconnoiter the area and report back their findings. These scouts climbed out of the Jordan valley and scoured the hills and streams of the land, probably traveling by night and hiding during the daylight hours.

It was a rich and fertile country in comparison to the dreary desert they had been through. They could hear the sounds of brooks, and glimpse rich pastureland; they were entranced by huge clusters of grapes glinting in the moonlight. As they flitted past encampments and fortifications, however, they caught sight of the inhabitants, and the promised land began to look a little less attractive. The tribes that were wandering over that area looked unusually tough and ugly, and more than one of the scouts began to have second thoughts about taking over the land.

They returned to Moses and the Israelites with two very different reports. The Bible gives a vivid picture of this reconnaissance party staggering into the encampment, loaded down with huge clusters of grapes slung on a pole between two men, and other samples of the fruit of the land. Caleb and Joshua said, "We went into the land to which you sent us. It does indeed flow with milk and honey; this is its produce. We must march in and conquer this land; we are well able to do it."

The other ten scouts however, delivered the alarmist, doomsaying view: "We are not able to march against this people; they are stronger than we are. The country . . . devours its inhabitants. Every man we saw there was of enormous size . . . We saw giants there [the sons of Anak, descendents of the Giants]. We felt like grasshoppers, and so we seemed to them."

The Israelites heeded the alarmist opinion and decided not to cross the river to take their promised land. Instead, they passed another *forty years* in the wilderness, until a new generation came forward and courageously entered under the leadership of Joshua.

A NEW VIEW OF RISK

The element of danger seems almost intrinsic to the word "risk." At least by definition it means "the possibility of loss or injury," "a dangerous element or factor," and "a dangerous chance." We could argue, however—and I believe rightly—that this is another of those words (similar to "crisis" and ""conflict") whose negative connotation has become definitive of the concept itself. People generally consider "crisis" to be an undesirable experience, when in fact it is actually a turning point in experience: a turning point possibly for the worse, yes; but also a turning point, possibly for the better. People generally fear "conflict"—some will do virtually anything to avoid it. It is indeed true that conflict can literally destroy people; but it cannot be denied that conflict can actually serve to bring people together into tighter bonding.

Likewise, risk continues to be associated only with negative images and possibilities. The colloquialisms associated with this "definition" are graphic and picturesque: to risk is to "go out on a limb," "tempt Providence," "sleep on a volcano," "dance on the razor's edge," "carry too much sail," "lay oneself open to," and "take one's life in one's hand." With such a company of witnesses as these, it is little wonder that most of us continue to perceive risk as negative and awesome.

If we are willing to expand our perception we can move beyond our cultural image of risk and perceive it as the experience of *choice* rather than a prelude to danger and trouble. We determined early on that our journey inward was designed to increase our self-knowledge and self-awareness. The journey into shadow accomplishes that quite successfully as long as we are willing to see our discoveries and are open to accept them as part of ourselves. The old axiom remains true: We can do nothing about that of which we are unaware. Increasing our self-knowledge and self-awareness brings into consciousness much new material, so that we are now faced with the matter of what to do with it.

Every increase in self-awareness generates a situation of choice that did not exist prior to the insight. Suppose we discover the live presence of envy in the mire of our shadow, and come to realize that our relationships have been affected by our unconscious projection of it onto others. This new insight now presents us with a choice. We may choose to act positively on the insight or deny its truth and reassign it to shadow. We may identify with it and consciously live it out through resentment and harsh judgment of others, and overt covetousness of what they have. We may study our envy to find its golden potential; or we may fall into deep despair, bemoaning our state of wretchedness.

Suppose we discover that there is hidden within us a kind, charitable, and accepting person who is quite the opposite of our stern, demanding, and somewhat legalistic conscious personality. We are now faced with the hard choice of what to do with this new insight. Shall we identify completely with it and become the precise opposite of what we were (and become a pushover for every manipulative personality we encounter)? Shall we embrace this newly discovered dimension of self and work to integrate it slowly into our existing persona? Shall we disown it, deny it, and cast it down into the depths of shadow? What shall be our choice?

We dare not make the mistake of thinking that every new insight from our Golden Shadow will be met with open arms and great rejoicing. Quite the contrary. People sometimes throw up their arms in despair, bemoaning their discovery, wailing, "I was better off before, even in my ignorance!" I once counseled with an attorney who lamented his discovery of a compassionate shadow opposite to his hard-nosed persona. "How can I go into court now," he repined, "and hammer away at my adversary, when I feel this sense of compassion that has suddenly come upon me?"

Or suppose the "long-lost" artist we had to repress and deny when we were a little child—because we were persuaded to believe that "painting is a waste of time," "there's no money in it," and "besides, artists are weird people"—is now clearly alive within us. Do we smile and embrace this newly discovered potential, or do we turn it away once again saying, "Oh, I could never learn to paint. People would just laugh at my efforts"?

Our work in bringing elements of our Golden Shadow into consciousness thus provides us with choices at the threshold of every new discovery. It is our responsibility to act on those options; for even *not* to act is itself a choice and therefore an action. This action, which is demanded by our new awareness, is the essence of risk. *Choosing is risking, and risking is choosing.*

It will do us no good to complain that we were "better off" before our journey inward and our discovery of our Golden Shadow. In the depth of our consciousness, we know better. The complaint is simply one of our ways to try to deal with the sometimes agonizing need to come to a decision and make our choice. We know that we can no longer go on blithely about our business as we were; but what are we to do?

THE CHOICE OF CHANGE

We are faced with the decision to choose the status quo or to choose change. Denying the insight of new awareness not only defeats the purpose of our journey inward, but also casts a vote to retain the status quo. Choosing to retain the status quo, once we "know better," is the choice that turns out to be the greatest risk of all. The *greatest* risk is *not* to risk, for it is to step out of the process of life and sit it out; to ride in the wagon, rather than to take up the reins and drive the horse.

The truth is that *all* of life is a series of risks, one after the other, from birth through to our final breath. Taking risks is inevitable; we cannot mature without it. The taking of risks early in life must, of course, be balanced with the protection of those who know much more about the reality of life than we, as infants, do. Our parents are our first guardians. They give us protective guidelines such as, "Don't ever do so and so," and "You must always be sure to do such and such." We are saved from doing harm to ourselves as well as to others if we will just obey. If our parents do even a reasonably adequate job of fulfilling this parental responsibility, we will usually agree with their judgment without much consideration.

As we grow up, this guardianship gradually but consistently decreases. Sometimes people refer to this in terms of giving up or surrendering the possession of more and more of the child as the child grows in maturity. Another way to perceive the process is to declare that as times goes on, parents progressively turn more and more of the responsibility for the child over to the child. Maturity is often reckoned against the yardstick of independence from parental guidance, support, and protection. This is nothing other than to separate from the known and the familiar and to lay aside our dependence. We do this gradually, choice by choice; and each choice is a risk.

Many parents, however, have a conscious or unconscious urge to keep their child dependent. When confronted with this observation, parents will often defend their overprotection by continuing to say things that were appropriate in early childhood, but certainly not later in the child's maturity. "We only want the best for you," and "We just don't want to see you get hurt" are fairly typical expressions of such an attitude. It is not unusual for parents to expect, either overtly or covertly, that their benevolent "rules" be obeyed as long as they live. Some parents control their children even from beyond the grave. Occasionally, adults still behave in accordance with parents' expectations long after their parents are dead.

But this is only part of the total picture. In the process of growing up most of us undoubtedly learned many lessons that were designed to prevent our taking risks. No doubt much of that learning was for our good, for as children and particularly as adolescents we develop the notion that we are indestructible and will live forever. We were, therefore, conditioned "not to take chances," and our positive response to that conditioning assured our acceptance by parents, and thus got our needs met and our wants fulfilled.

Conditioning, however, may go far beyond its intended borders. We may readily repeat behaviors that brought satisfaction and reward long after any satisfaction or reward is to be gained. We may continue to repeat these behaviors even if they now work against us.

RATIONALIZATION AND RISKING

Old directives and perceptions regarding risk-taking may be yet another potential saboteur of our task of acting on the insights from our Golden Shadow, and endeavoring to fulfill our undeveloped self. There are indeed outer voices, as well as inner voices, that are alarmist by nature with doomsaying as their proclamation. While we may consciously accept the fact that risk-taking is essential to the experience of life, we still must face what appears to be the "reasonableness of playing it safe" at the discovery of every new possibility. Despite "knowing better," we can easily talk ourselves out of acting on our discoveries and justify our decision with a host of "reasons."

Somewhere within our maturing process we develop a collection of various defense and coping mechanisms that serve unconsciously to protect us from threats to our sense of safety and security. One of the most readily employed of these mechanisms is rationalization. Those who use rationalization often support it by saying that it is only reasonable. Rationalization, however, differs from reasoning in that it only selects those facts and factors that promise a desired, already determined conclusion or solution. Rationalization then, is the conscious justification of a decision after the decision has already been determined by unconscious motivation.

Rationalization arises out of the inner voices that say, "Watch out," "Be careful," "Are you sure you want to do this?" and "Is it worth it? " Rationalization "talks down" risk-taking by telling us that it will jeopardize our safety and security, and do we really want that to happen? If we risk by choosing change we leave the certain for the uncertain. If we depart from the status quo, we leave the known and the experienced for the unknown and the unexperienced. Rationalization will try to help us see the "impropriety" of risk and will put up a strong argument for its rejection.

The mechanism of rationalization *can* be our friend; more often than not, however, it encourages us to pull the wool over our eyes and fail to see clearly the reality that is before us. The fact is that *there is no absolute security in this life. We live on faith and hope.* Certainly we do as much as is reasonable to provide for our safety and security, *but in the end there is no guarantee that all our efforts will have made any difference at all.* This is not a declaration of defeatism or nihilism; it is merely a report of reality.

Rather than seeking to preserve safety and security at all costs, we are encouraged to experience a vulnerability that is the precise opposite. It is within this vulnerability that the greatest development of our undeveloped self takes place. Risk, then, far from being avoided, needs to be the order of the day; we see once again that the greatest risk, truly, is *not* to risk.

THE ELEMENT OF VULNERABILITY

One of the colloquialisms cited earlier to "define" risk was "to lay oneself open to." This is precisely the concept of vulnerability, and is a wonderfully positive, potentiality-developing statement. We allow openness within ourselves; we lower our guard and drop our defenses. We mellow; we let the past be the past; and we give consideration to the new possibilities that present themselves. We allow "I would never" slowly to become, "I guess I can."

I grew up with a stepmother who hated cats. I irrationally adopted this attitude as my own and retained it for nearly fifty years. In fact, it was only after getting our third consecutive cat (long after my stepmother's death) that I allowed myself to be open to the possibility of liking a cat. While this may appear on the surface to be a relatively insignificant change, it was for me a meaningful experience that demonstrated both the depth and strength of resistance to risking change, as well as the reality of living out a possibility in spite of stubborn resistance.

We make ourselves vulnerable in choosing to live out the potential brought forth from our Golden Shadow. We see the actual desirability of this vulnerability and we are encouraged to act. We also realize, however, that rejection by the outer world is still a very real possibility and this may very well dampen our enthusiasm to risk. We find ourselves right back in the situation of our prior experience, when we repressed many of these potentials into our shadow because they were rejected by the outer world.

In 1969, John Powell wrote *Why Am I Afraid to Tell You who I Am?*, a book on self-awareness and personal growth. While writing the book, he asked a person the title question. The person replied, "I am afraid to tell you who I am, because if I tell you who I am, you may not like who I am, and it's all that I have."

There is nothing to be gained by denying the possibility that the outer world will reject our living out of the attributes of our rediscovered and uncovered self. Rejection is always a potential consequence of the vulnerability of risk-taking. Acceptance, however, is equally a potential consequence; and at this milepost on our journey, we focus our attention on the positive possibilities.

SELF-IMAGE AND RISK-TAKING

Positive self-image develops firm self-confidence and thus provides courage to risk. One of the many by-products of our journey inward is the realization of ourselves as people of substance. We *do* have personal strength. In our spiritual dimension, we see the support and strength of God permeating our whole experience of life. Therefore, we do not fear being "blown away" by a possible rejection by the outer world.

This is not cockiness, vanity, or empty boasting. It is a quiet affirmation of what we know to be true. Nor is the risk-taking synonymous with recklessness, as it is so often in adolescence or irresponsible adulthood. This risk-taking is *never an end unto itself;* it has purpose, dream, vision, objective, and goal.

The primary and most frequent complaint of people moving into the later years of life is, "I did not take enough risks." This is spoken out of the perfect vision of hindsight, with a sort of plaintive longing that suggests, "I wish I had." I have observed over many years, however, that people are often much more *aware* of potentials in their Golden Shadow than they realize or want to realize. The reluctance to risk living them out is strong enough to keep these elements just below the level of consciousness; but they are easily brought to the fore. This is true particularly of undeveloped potential in the realm of occupation.

For instance, many people who experience a vague dissatisfaction or sense of unfulfillment with their occupation already know what they would prefer to be doing with their lives. Some do not know they know, but are nevertheless able to bring into consciousness very quickly a desired alternative occupation that has been resident in their shadow for who knows how long.

If I say to such a person, "If someone were to give you a blank check, and tell you to write in whatever it is that you really want to do or be occupationally, what would you write?" The reaction is usually quite similar from person to person. The person will smile almost immediately—a rather sheepish smile—and then quickly answer the question with virtually no hesitation. Their countenance lightens and there is a tone of excitement in their voice.

When I once asked this of a computer programmer, he grinned and quickly replied, "I would dearly love to have my own pet shop." This man was as much an outdoorsman as a whiz at programming. Doing something related to animals was his hidden "dream." An attorney once told me, "I would like very much to write; in fact, I would like to write religious literature." I once asked this question of a physician. She immediately broke into a broad grin and with no hesitation said, "I'd operate a Dairy Queen!" This was a gregarious, energetic woman who liked dealing with people; but she preferred dealing with them in a much different way.

In virtually all the stories recounted in this book the people who chose to live out and fulfill the potentials of their Golden Shadow did so by risking—by taking chances. They were not, however, spur-of-the-moment, impulsive actions. They were thought through and planned. Some of the people took great risk; some took small risks. Tim, the ex-social worker who became a computer programmer, had to borrow a considerable sum of money to finance his training. Patricia, the woman who once had suffered shame and self-rejection, put herself at substantial risk pursuing the profession of attorney. She had no guarantee that she would not backslide into her "unacceptable self" and thus become ineffective as a lawyer. Michael, the junior high school math teacher, took a big risk in leaving his job to pursue an uncertain future as an author of children's stories.

All these people thought through the ramifications of fulfilling their newly discovered potential. They considered as many sides of the choices as they were able. Their conclusions were essentially to "do it," rather than to join the ranks of those who in later years would say, "I wish I had taken more risks."

FREEDOM TO RISK IN THE LATER YEARS

Sometimes people fear they are too old to risk living out the discovered potentials of the golden shadow. This fear, however, is to forget our earlier observation that human maturation continues until our death. We can remain open to the surprises of our golden shadow and endeavor to exploit them as long as there is breath in our body. In fact, the willingness to be open to new possibilities and to risk acting them out may even prove to be directly related to longevity.

Examples abound. Harland Sanders, known to us as Colonel Sanders of Kentucky Fried Chicken, began to franchise his chicken recipe when he was sixty-six years old. Harriet Doerr wrote her first novel, *Stones for Ibarra*, at age seventy-four , and received the 1984 American Book Award for it. Anna Mary Robertson Moses, known to us fondly as Grandma Moses, never touched a paint brush until she was in her late seventies. She became a widely known and highly popular artist and remained as such until her death in 1961 at the age of 101 years.

One of the tragedies of living is to believe it is too late to risk the experience of change. Those people moving into the later years of life who complain that they "did not take enough risks" only compound their distress if they believe that it is now too late to do so. "The train has already left the depot," they say. Perhaps. But there are trains that depart regularly every hour on the hour. Every day of our lives, no matter what our situation, we are presented with the opportunity to risk change and development—movement to a greater realization of all that we can be. The opportunity is there if we will but grasp it. We need not think in terms of gigantic leaps or phenomenal transformations; no matter how small, how tiny, how infinitesimal the risk, *taking it* is the blood of life that vivifies our being.

Just as there is the initial fear and hesitation to begin the journey inward, there is the similar reluctance to live out our discoveries and seek to fulfill the potential of our Golden Shadow. There is always an alarmist attitude both within and without that will endeavor to discourage us from risking. Nevertheless, with firm trust in ourselves and in the Spirit of God within us, we take our lives into our hands and control our destiny. We know there is often the trade-off—that we must surrender A to take up B; that we must leave C to go to D; that we have to stop doing or being E in order to do or be F. We use the power of meditation to visualize vividly, in great detail, the many facets of ourselves we will risk developing. We experience the internal courage to reconstruct the future as we now visualize it.

In the last analysis, our willingness to risk living out the potential of our Golden Shadow rests on our acceptance of the innate wisdom of the act itself.

CHAPTER 11

The Value of Failure

During the academic year 1988–89, the University of Michigan Business School in Ann Arbor offered for the first time a course titled, "Failure 101." Jack Matson, a professor of engineering from the University of Houston, taught the course under the visiting professorship of the Zell-Laurie Fellowship of the university. The course, intended to foster the skills of entrepreneurship and build self-confidence through reality-facing, was based on a series of "hurdle-jumping" exercises that confronted the students with repeated failures.

Such education is appropriate, not only in business school, but in the general experience of everyday life. Failure is an ever-present reality. Many people were undoubtedly surprised to see a course listed as "Failure 101" in a university catalogue; just as it may at first seem strange to see a chapter titled "The Value of Failure" in a book such as this with its positive, uplifting orientation.

Contrary to popular belief, failure has much to offer and is something from which we may learn. This is particularly true for those of us on our journey of endeavoring to live out and fulfill the discoveries in our Golden Shadow. Most of us still struggle with an image of failure that is more damaging than helpful. We are unwilling to accept failure as a reasonable, even necessary part of existence—something from which we can learn, and something which can prove to be valuable to us.

In doing the literature research for this book, I came upon a volume in the public library written by Dr. Robert T. Lewis, titled, *Taking Chances: The Psychology of Losing and How To Profit From It.* Chapter 14 of the book is titled, "The Myth of Perfection," and is the author's attempt to help us realize the normalcy of our imperfection and thus be enabled to accept ourselves in the experiences and events of failure. Apparently, however, this was too much to ask of one reader, for scrawled in bold capital letters across the bottom of the last page of the chapter were the words, "BE PERFECT AS YOUR HEAVENLY FATHER IS PERFECT! MATTHEW 5:48."

Whoever wrote the message was simply not willing to accept Lewis's statements about the omnipresent reality of imperfection among human beings, and how our awareness and acceptance of this fact could be extremely helpful in enabling us to accept failure as normal. Not so, said the scrawler. People—at least godly people—must be perfect, as God is perfect; there is no room for imperfection!

The irony rests in the words of the Bible verse chosen by the critic to refute Lewis's statements. The Greek word, which in the Matthew 5:48 verse is usually translated "perfect," literally means "wanting nothing necessary for completeness" and implies what we would today refer to as "wholeness" and "completeness." Our understanding of wholeness and completeness necessarily *includes all dimensions of our being,* not the least of which is our multifaceted imperfection.

THE PLACE OF SUCCESS AND FAILURE IN SOCIETY

This person's denial of failure is reflective of a society that has a generally warped perception of failure and success. Society in general, and most subcultures, promote success to the exclusion of failure. Failure is highly unacceptable, and may actually be punished severely be the subculture. Positive regard or acceptance of failure has no place in public and must be relegated to the shadow. We learn that failure is a dark and sinister element we must avoid at all costs, keep out of sight, and not even discuss.

Success, on the other hand, is so highly honored that it is generally more respected than even the characteristics of honesty and kindness. It is such a dominant, powerful, and influential standard in society and most subcultures that people will often abandon other standards such as integrity, truthfulness, and honesty for the sake of success. It is not uncommon for people to cheat, lie, and steal in order to be successful. The rewards and payoffs for success are enormous, and most people are highly motivated to achieve it.

The mythos surrounding success and failure is a powerful teacher and developer of our values, standards, and personalities. In some subcultures, success may be virtually deified, while failure is condemned. At any and all cost, success must be achieved and failure avoided. While success is regarded as the fundamental goal of life ("In all things be successful"), failure is considered an unforgivable sin, and forms a potential eleventh commandment: "Thou shalt not fail."

We can hardly escape this indoctrination in the developmental process. These messages are given both overtly and covertly. We develop in a milieu that daily screams out the reward for success in a score of ways, and quietly baits, seduces, and cajoles us into idolizing it; while at the same time it blatantly denounces failure as a defect, and surreptitiously and subtly punishes it.

In our endeavor to become what we can be, this mythos can negatively influence or even prevent our willingness to risk living out facets of our potential. We are often so afraid of failing that we become intimidated or rendered powerless in our attempt to act on insights brought to our consciousness from the Golden Shadow. Much like John Powell's respondent, we may query, "What if I share with you the true, authentic person that I am, and you don't like it? What then? Do I want to risk that rejection—that failure? I want you to like who I am, and maybe you won't. That would be a terrible failure."

More often than not, it is enough of a task to begin to live out our newly discovered potentials, let alone have to deal with fears about the outcomes. Therefore, we must somehow demythologize the perception of society and reevaluate the image and place of failure.

FAILURE DEMYTHOLOGIZED

Failure is a judgment or assessment of experiences, events, and efforts. Failure is an opinion, and as such always carries with it a degree of subjectivity. Experiences, events, and efforts are just that; they are neither successes nor failures until a judgment or assessment is made of them and an opinion rendered. More often than not, the judgment is in the mind of the perceiver. What appears to be a success to one person may be judged a failure by another.

A classic cold war story establishes this point clearly. A Russian and an American ran a race. The American was the first to cross the finish line and so won the race. Following the victory, an American newspaper heralded the result with a headline that read, "American Wins Race; Russian Finishes Last." The Russian newspaper headline proclaimed, "Russian Places Second in Race; American Is Next to Last." Both observations were, of course, precisely correct.

Furthermore, *we* are not the experience, event, or effort—unless, of course, we choose to identify ourselves completely with them. Remember Albert, the manager of the medical clinic? In his perception, he and the smooth operation of the clinic were one. If the clinic failed to operate smoothly under his direction and management, he, Albert, would be a failure. His statement would be, "I am a failure," not "The experience of managing failed," or "The event of management failed," or "The efforts to manage failed."

When we refuse to identify with the experience, we are not dodging responsibility or projecting it elsewhere. We are simply clarifying perception so the experience may become a learning experience rather than a self-destructive one. If Albert were to continue to perceive himself as a failure, he would very well be crippled or at least severely handicapped in ever seeing himself again as a productive person. This is how some people become perpetually unsuccessful at all they do—they develop a perception of themselves as "failures." If we believe we *are* failures, then the system of self-fulfilling prophecy will go into effect, and we will live out the assessment. Whatever we touch will fail because we expect it to and believe it will. Fear of future failures, obviously, will be an effective detriment to any efforts to live out undeveloped potentials from our Golden Shadow.

To perceive failure as a judgment or assessment of experiences, events, and efforts is, however, contrary to what most of us have learned. "You" phrases are usually more the order of the day: "You are stupid," "You can't do anything right," "You are nothing but trouble," "You are a loser." It is extremely important to see the gross error of such absolutizing and the destructive effect it may have on our self-image and self-confidence. It is necessary for us to replace that judgment of self with the judgment of experience and efforts. We can do this only if we have loved and accepted ourselves as we are, as creations of great worth and value.

As human beings we are a complex composite of thousands of accomplishments, aptitudes, ideas, and talents. To consider our whole life to be a failure because of one or two experiences of failure in one or two of those many facets is to "catastrophize" those experiences well out of proportion to their significance. Often we assign arbitrary weight and importance to certain efforts or events and then use these chosen ones as yardsticks to measure our worth. This selectivity is clearly unfair to ourselves, even though we may argue that those items of experience or effort selected as criteria are of utmost importance. Our life is not a failure because we did not receive the promotion. Our life is not a failure because we did not win the race, or pass the course. Our life is not a failure because someone we hoped would like us, doesn't. It would be extremely difficult to defend the "catastrophic" position that the evaluation of our entire life depends upon the success or failure of any one or two or even dozen experiences or efforts. It simply is not so.

SUCCESS AND FAILURE ARE RELATIVE

If we are to be free from the potential paralyzing effect of fearing failure, it will be necessary to reevaluate success and failure as we commonly valued them. We observed earlier that most of us develop without giving much conscious consideration to values—we simply adopt them as our own, uncritically, as they are offered to us. We need to review our values now to determine if the ultimate importance of success and the grave dread of failure are values we truly hold as our own at this precise time, or whether they are carryovers from previous indoctrinations.

Priorities do change with the passage of time. What was once important, even critical, may be far from that now. What was taboo may now be sought after. The undesirable becomes the desirable, and vice versa. We may choose to play tennis now simply for the fun of the sport and the benefit of exercise, rather than to *win*. Is it a failure, then, not to be able to serve every ball with the velocity of a speeding bullet? If we play simply to experience the thrill of competition, we may be a failure by Wimbledon's standards, but a success by our own.

The person who responded to John Powell's question about telling others who we really are would experience success whether the other person liked him or not. The purpose of sharing ourselves authentically with another person is to be able to do it—to present ourselves as we are rather than to pretend to be something other. Once we do that, we cannot fail, regardless of that other person's acceptance or rejection. Of course, most of us would prefer to be accepted rather than rejected by others, and that is reasonable. But if we endeavor to be our true self rather than a phony, *that* is the success. Even being rejected by the other person does not constitute a failure.

Unless we reevaluate society's standards of success and failure for ourselves, and review our perception of them, we may make mistakes in assessing our efforts to act upon and live out the discoveries in our undeveloped self. We may erroneously see our effort as a failure, when in fact it is a great success.

THE DEBUT OF NEW FEATURES

Our established persona elements are cultured and slick, sophisticated, and refined. Their edges have been smoothed and their corners rounded by possibly decades of use in interaction with the outer world. Aptitudes have become skilled through years of practice. By contrast, the newly discovered, emerging shadow elements are rough, unsophisticated, crude, and possibly undisciplined. They are awkward and perhaps even bumbling. They need time to adjust to the light. It is important to remember that our persona characteristics once existed in quite the same fashion as these newly emerging shadow traits; they, too, needed to be developed. Time and use have made them appropriate and dignified. Time and use will do the same for our newly discovered dimensions.

We can learn to be patient with ourselves and accept and love ourselves in the process of living out the discoveries of the Golden Shadow. We know we are doing what we want to do, and we will succeed. If we should unearth a proclivity for, let us say, playing the flute, and we are excited by this discovery, we will undoubtedly seek someone to teach us how to play it. We probably will not expect ourselves to be able to play brilliantly after one week's lessons. In the same manner, then, we do not entertain the unreasonable expectations that other dimensions of discovery will be immediately assimilated into our consciousness and present themselves as seasoned performers. If we are in any way rejected by others in the process of our "redevelopment," we do not view this as failure; we simply remind ourselves that in our earlier development we probably experienced the same thing.

We may also worry that our emerging shadow element may obliterate our persona. But our fears of this happening are often greatly exaggerated. Remember the attorney in the previous chapter, who feared that his new-found compassion would cause him to lose his edge in the heated tension of the courtroom? He need not have worried; for the conscious expression of this new-found trait caused him little embarrassment with its awkwardness and unsophistication. Rightly so, he did not identify completely with this emergence of compassion and become the opposite of his "old self." On the contrary, in a relatively short time it had become integrated into his personality; it provided him with a new richness of understanding of human beings, and led him to be a little less "deaf" to what others had to say.

THE HIDDEN BENEFITS OF FAILURE

Most of us are unmotivated to look for any benefits in failure. Since failure is generally considered to be so undesirable, how could it possibly be beneficial?

Failure can actually build self-confidence if it teaches us that we can "roll with the punches," be resilient, and survive defeat. Most people, however, look at failure and see it as erosive of self-confidence. This is true only if we have failed to separate ourselves from the experience, effort, or event.

Only by risking failure can we accomplish anything. We can sit on the bench and declare that if we ever picked up a bat, we could knock the ball out of the park. But until we step up to the plate and risk striking out, we will never know if that statement is truth or fantasy.

By analyzing failure we can learn from our mistakes. Business students study the history of companies that have failed. Entrepreneurs who go bankrupt examine their assumptions and performance: Did we misjudge the marketplace? Did we overestimate what we could produce? Did we underestimate our capital needs? Did we discount the competition? Learning from their mistakes prevents a repeat performance.

There are groups of professionals who come together regularly to recount their failures. They identify what new knowledge they gained from those failures and help colleagues save time by telling them what *doesn't* work. "We tried so and so, and that didn't work, so there's no use in your wasting your time on so and so."

The world of scientific experimentation probably best understands the perception of failure we have been considering in this chapter: Failure is the assessment or judgment of an effort, experience, or event. Scientific laboratories are the arenas of countless failures and the wearying process of trial and error as scientists seek their discoveries. When an experiment proves fruitless, the scientist perceives it as an incomplete result, not a failure. It is the outcome of personal efforts; the result of the event (experiment). Failure is often the price of ultimate success.

We cannot isolate ourselves from the possibility of failure if we are at all serious about our quest for the Golden shadow. We will experience failure just as surely as the sun will rise in the east and set in the west. If we prefer a protective greenhouse existence wherein we will not have to risk failure, we can never expect to move toward being what we can be. Only through the experience of failure can we know what success is.

If we choose to listen to those three complaints made by people who are moving into the later years of life, we will take more risks, knowing there is always the possibility of failure, but confident, also, of being able to accept it, should it happen, knowing that we can even learn from it. Perhaps this is what the number one complaint is really saying: "Don't hesitate to take your risks, for, after all, even if it 'doesn't work' (and you fail), which is better to say: 'I made a mistake,' or 'I wish I had tried'?"

CHAPTER 12

The Excitement of Creating

In 1929, President Herbert Hoover appointed a commission to develop a futurist vision that would help the United States plot its course thorough the next twenty-five years. In time, the commission fulfilled its assignment and reported its findings to Franklin D. Roosevelt, who was then president. The report was comprised of thirteen volumes, prepared by five hundred researchers. The summary of the report alone totaled 1,600 pages. Yet there was no mention of jet propulsion, atomic energy, antibiotics, transistors, or several other significant developments that had occurred by 1954.

The great World's Fair of 1939, dedicated to the World of Tomorrow, likewise failed to suggest any of these advances, and even overlooked the concept of space travel. Meanwhile, Alex Raymond, creator of the comic strip "Flash Gordon," had been depicting his characters involved in interplanetary adventures since 1934.

People such as Alex Raymond and Chester Gould, creator of the comic strip "Dick Tracy," were fantastic dreamers who put their fantasies on paper. Dick Tracy was using his two-way wrist radio way back in the 1930s. These people were uninhibited by researchers and committees; they simply let loose their creative imagination. Jules Verne's fantastic perceptions in *Twenty Thousand Leagues Under the Sea* turned out to be far more prophetically accurate than many official predictions.

A NEW WAY OF THINKING

Creativity demands of us a new way of thinking. It requires freedom from the bonds of rationality. We must, of course, hold fast to rationality for the living of our lives, else the result would be probable chaos.

But when we contemplate creativity, we move into a different atmosphere altogether, wherein the irrational is the desired, even essential, norm.

The Industrial Revolution was responsible for upsetting Thomas Malthus's doomsaying prediction of 1798, that the discrepancy between food production and population growth would lead to worldwide starvation. Malthus was so caught up in rational mathematical calculations that he failed to include the irrational elements of human creativity, ingenuity, inventiveness, and innovation.

Creativity suggests that, for a time, we abandon "common sense," that ancient pillar of homespun truth and wisdom. Common sense is valuable, but it may stifle creativity. If we adhered to common sense, we would still believe the sun orbits around the earth; for common sense tells us as we watch it "rise" in the east, "move" across the sky, and "set" in the west, that *it* is in motion and we are fixed in place. Common sense tells us that a massive vehicle made out of metal cannot possibly fly in the air. Furthermore, it would be ludicrous to shape a boat hull out of concrete, because common sense tells us that concrete dropped into water goes straight to the bottom. To be creative, it is important to challenge common sense.

This may be easier said than done; for we are quite naturally stuck in reality, tending to see reality the way it appears. We continue to see things the way we have always known them. We have been taught from early on that our intellectual, rational, reasoning self should dominate. This is generally the essence of our formal and informal training. We are rarely taught to be irrationally creative; on the contrary, this is more often than not discouraged. We continue, then, through most of our lives to see things the way we have always known them. To become creative, however, we free our minds from this traditional way of thinking; for the creative process is very often the opposite of logic.

J. R. R. Tolkien reminds us of this when he says, "What really happens is that the story-maker proves a successful 'sub-creator.' He makes a Secondary World which your mind can enter. Inside it, what he relates is 'true'; it accords with the laws of that world. You therefore believe it, while you are, as it were, inside."

We cannot be creative if we are compelled to remain lodged in our usual, standard patterns, paradigms, and configurations. We must move beyond them, outside of them, outside the boundaries of our structured process of thinking. If we believe we are dealing with facts, we free ourselves enough to perceive that we are often dealing with widely held beliefs that may be altered. We distinguish between concrete facts and likely probabilities. Likely probabilities contain possibilities that concrete facts can never offer. Creativity thrives in the realm of possibility. It is somewhat difficult to develop creativity around the arithmetic equation $2 + 2 = 4$. There is, however, considerable room for creativity in the equation, Wealth = Power, for this is not a fact but a probability.

Consequently, we consider what seem like strange ways of thinking. Our rational minds wants to cling to forms of neat order, and we brush aside this tendency for the sake of creativity. We move from the orderly, precise, analytical thought of everyday life into "inexact thought" (near thought, proximate thought). We shift from literal to metaphorical and associative thinking—a kind of thinking that is midway between rationality and deep meditation. Metaphors are those marvelous, nonliteral figures of speech wherein a word or phrase that denotes one kind of idea or object is used in place of another to suggest an analogy or likeness between them. We think of a computer having senses and a memory; we speak of a ship plowing the waves of the sea; we consider the earth as God's footstool. In our creative mode we move away from the literal, and refuse to be bound by rationality. Creative thought is perhaps even closer to the meditative state than to rational cognition.

The intuitive function of our personality is very helpful in the process of creating, because it focuses more on opportunities and *possibilities* than on what is. It seeks to apprehend the widest range of possibilities, consistently asking, "What are the possibilities of this objective situation?" Intuition endeavors to "see" what is not yet, but what will or can come to be.

Intuition perceives, through the unconscious, realities not yet known to consciousness. The intuitive function touches the archetypes of the collective unconscious and perceives relationships there. Through this function we may experience precognition—seeing the handwriting on the wall. Thus intuition goes far beyond the customary, beyond the familiar, the known, and the well-established.

Intuition prefers to make decisions based on human values and personal feelings even if those decisions cannot be logically described or founded in fact. It operates in terms of figurative language, symbols, imagination, and illusions. It is expectant, inventive, and original. Intuition likes to solve problems by playing hunches.

THE RESOURCE OF THE UNCONSCIOUS

We have come to see the unconscious as a vast storehouse of all that has gone on before. It is not surprising, then, that it should provide a tremendous resource for creativity. We tap into the images that are in our memories, our preconscious, our personal unconscious, and the collective unconscious. We explore the elements of our life experience, all that we have learned, accumulated, and stored away.

In the process of creating we access our unconscious in a variety of ways. In meditation we guide ourselves in imagery associated with the subject of our creating. We press out new ideas and perceptions from the unconscious by changing the attributes of the subject on which we are thinking. We make "hot" into "cold," "stubborn" into "pliable," "stationary" into "free-floating." We constantly seek *possibilities* that can or may be, but are not.

We may think of something quite other than what we're thinking and working on. We "take a break" from the matter before us, and shift to another consideration. From this, we bring in new data that may be quite unrelated to our current subject of thought to see if this can in any way enhance it or give it new perspective.

We free-associate, allowing our mind to skip from one consideration to another, particularly in illogical skips.

We pay attention to our dreams, being open to creative ideas expressed in unusual forms and symbols. We look for resolutions when we are stuck or deadlocked, at a standstill in our process of creating. Solutions seem to emerge from the unconscious particularly in the hours preceding awaking.

This story is told of Elias Howe, one of the inventors of the sewing machine. In 1843, he struggled with the problem of developing an appropriate needle for the little device that would take the thread through the material without going all the way through itself. He had no success, until one night he "discovered" the solution in a dream. In the dream, he was pursued by cannibals in Africa. As they got closer and closer, he could see that they all had spears shaped like sewing needles. Suddenly, he tripped and fell, and the cannibals hovered over him with their spears raised, ready to thrust them into him. Howe looked up and saw at the top of one of the spears the precise kind of eye that was necessary for his sewing machine needle. After the dream, he fashioned that needle, which—in combination with a shuttle below—solved his problem.

THE DISCOMFORT FACTOR IN CREATIVITY

The journey inward often confronts us with the anguish and agony of our lives. We have seen that coming to grips with our shadow is hardly something to be desired, but definitely something that needs to be done. In order to climb the mountain, we must pass through the valley, and that is painful. It is extremely difficult to turn around and look inward, and so we put it off until we know intuitively that we can no longer. What we see then compels us finally to confess to ourselves that the root of the bulk of our "troubles" of life is really not "out there" somewhere, but right "in here." Nevertheless, we have seen that it is in embracing our darkness that we find new light. This is an ever-repeating cycle—possibly the essence of our journey, to the end of this aspect of life.

It is out of this experience that creativity may arise. Creativity and contentment are incompatible. People who are quite comfortable in their lives are generally not known for their creativity. Many creative types appear to have experienced stress and trauma in their lives to a more significant degree than others. For example, many people (particularly writers) who have experienced the death of one or both of their parents early in life are creative types. Possibly the trauma of the death causes some children to become achievement-oriented as a way of coping. People with certain mood disorders have long been noted to demonstrate high degrees of creativity. Relatives of such people, however, may also manifest creativity, even though they themselves experience only a mild form of the disorder, or even no evidence at all.

Creativity is not to be thought of as a straight line, "ever onward, ever upward." Much creativity arises out of the tension produced by failure. It is often a difficult struggle; we may go through a series of failures in the experience of creating before we achieve success. We try "this," and we try "that"; but we know when we have the "right one." Many writers describe their experience of creating as a struggle to give birth to ideas and concepts, and articulate them with both clarity and impact. For many, it does not come easily, but requires diligent work.

We have already seen that the experience of living out the discovered dimensions of our Golden Shadow requires us to take risks and stretch ourselves. We reach beyond our grasp, and we risk failure each time we do it. It is, nevertheless, in this mind-set and atmosphere that creativity occurs.

OUR PROCESS IS A CREATIVE PROCESS

There is great similarity between the process of our work in bringing forward our Golden Shadow and the experience of creativity. We may confidently say that our experience is itself an act of great creativity. Creativity, we have noted, often comes out of thinking in terms of opposites. We have the subject, the pattern, the fact, the issue, the reality. Now, is there another way? Is there a better way? We look at and consider the opposite. We take this reality's opposite and translate it into a concept that develops a contradiction. We then resolve contradiction to create a new solution.

Creativity, then, is the recombination of what already exists—the synthesis of thesis and antithesis. Every great idea involves a unification of opposites, for this is the essence of the concept of wholeness and completeness.

When we review the path of our journey, we see clearly the creativity that is there. It is essentially a cycle of change. We began with an established persona—a system of characteristics, values, and actions; a way of being. This is commonly brought about by parents and our subculture. If this persona is continued beyond its period of usefulness and purposiveness, we become stagnated, frustrated, disenchanted, dissatisfied, rigid, lifeless, and out or sorts with everything.

In response, there will emerge a new potential value, trait, or aptitude out of our shadow. There will be opposites—contradictions, usually—of what previously existed in our persona. These new emergences are contradictory not only to our existing persona, but often to the standards of our subculture as well. There follows, then, an internal conflict that can only be settled by a conscious choice and decision of what to do with the newly emerged material. We fear risking the change, for we know it will be different. We fear the outcomes.

Nevertheless, we act on our insights, embrace and incorporate our discoveries into our conscious self, and experience beneficial recombination, reconstruction, and redevelopment of our personhood. Our reward is a new self that is neither the old nor its opposite, but the offspring of the union of the two—a new creation.

HOW WE MAY ENCOURAGE CREATIVITY

It is essential for us to realize that all forms of creativity can be exercised and developed. There are attitudes and actions that can enhance the potential in each of us and nourish the expression of our creativity.

We have already reviewed the foundational importance of a positive self-image and healthy self-esteem. Self-confidence can provide us with a positive, uplifting, and affirming attitude. Creativity requires that we be able to say "yes" and be "for," rather than saying "no" and being "against." "Possibility" is a key word in all creativity; therefore, we are open to a wide variety of possibilities, fantastic though some of them may be. We become excited about our creativity and thrill to the experience of bringing into being that which was not. The magnitude of creation is of much lesser significance than the excitement of creativity. We must plan to become deeply immersed in it, for creating requires time and uses time. We try to associate with like-minded people—people of the same attitude, who themselves are creative in a great variety of ways.

We need to be curious and investigative—like cats, who explore the world with their noses. We assist our imagination by looking for new pieces of information which may be used in generating new combinations. We visit places of creativity, read about creative individuals, and peruse books and magazines of creative themes. We pay attention to our surroundings and discover resources for our creative imagination to process. We perceive even the experience of ordinary, everyday life to be pregnant with *possibilities.*

One day a man watched college students amuse themselves by throwing metal pie pans back and forth to each other, instead of returning them to the Frisbee Pie Company. It occurred to him that this simple act had very real possibilities. He took his idea to the Wham-O Company, which modified the shape of the pans, molded a plastic replica, and produced millions of units. Thus was the Frisbee born.

In being positive and affirmative, we lay aside our fear of the unknown, of rejection, and of failure. Failure may be nothing more than one step to success. Thomas Edison originally invented the phonograph to be a "repeating station" for telephone calls. He believed that the telephone would be too costly for most people, therefore calls to individuals could come into a central location, be recorded, and held until the person came in to hear his or her call (as one might pick up mail at a post office). The concept of the repeating station was never very popular, but we all know the fabulous ongoing story of sound recording and reproduction created by Edison's invention.

Creativity needs a dream (or dreams). In Rogers and Hammerstein's musical *South Pacific*, Bloody Mary, an island native, sings the delightful song, "Happy Talk," to the young lovers; "You got to have a dream," she says. "If you don' have a dream; how you gonna have a dream come true?"

The voice of creativity is an inner voice, and we must listen to it to fulfill many of the potentials of our Golden Shadow. From time to time it speaks to us. Instead of pretending that we do not hear it, or ignoring it completely, we can pay close attention to it and follow its suggestions. The voice may be irrational. Instead of allowing our rational minds to shout it down with, "That is out of the question; I could never do that," we may pause reflectively and say, "Hm-m; that's an interesting possibility. It's certainly worth a try." From time to time we get glimpses of our potential for creativity. Instead of brushing them aside as so much fantasy—just as we used to brush aside cameo appearances of our dark shadow by saying, "I didn't see that"—we may examine them closely and look further into them. The creativity of our Golden Shadow holds up marvelous potentials for us to savor. We can smile somewhat sheepishly, cast our eyes down, twist our toe into the ground, and respond, "Oh yes, that would be wonderful; but I can't do that"; or we can beam with the joy of anticipation and respond, "Great; let's do it!"

So many people approach the later years of life in somewhat poignant melancholy, more in sadness than in anger, knowing that it is not so much that life has passed them by, but more that they have simply spent their days quietly watching life go by. "I wish I had taken more risks. I wish I had been more assertive." There is no better time than the present.

CHAPTER 13

Resolution and Determination

Discipline can be a difficult concept. Resolution and determination are ominous sounding words, and they are largely alien to much of our everyday living. We find an interesting account of resolution and determination (and the corresponding lack of it) in Lawrence Sanders's novel, *Caper*.

Caper is a fascinating story about Jannie Shean, an author of mystery-suspense thrillers. Jannie had come under fire from her publisher because her writing was "losing its edge" and she was out of touch with the reality of street crime. To resolve this problem and gain some street-wise experience, Jannie, along with her companion Dick Fleming, concocted the scheme of planning for a "caper"—the robbery of a Manhattan jewelry store accompanied by some true-to-life thieves whom they would hire. Their intention was to go through the whole process up to the point of the actual heist, and then pay off the robbers and call off the event.

Everything worked well, except that the hired burglars refused to abort the plan, and forced Jannie Shean and Dick Fleming to participate with them in the holdup. While sitting in the getaway car with the hoods, Jannie meditated on some disturbing thoughts.

I had another vagrant thought on that trip to the West 47th Street garage. It will probably make me sound like a snob, a prig, an elitist, whatever, but if this is to be a true and honest account, I must record it.

I thought that Dick Fleming and I were superior to these creatures. We were better informed, better educated, more intelligent, more sensitive. It was a matter of breeding, or class; yes, it was. We would never have chosen to associate with any one of them if it hadn't been for our harebrained scheme. Quite simply, they were beneath us.

Yet there we were, in the power of those inferior beings. Because they had shrewdness, strength, vigor, and *determination* that could not be denied. Most important, they were not daunted by action. I tried to recall an instance in my life in which I had planned and carried out a project of moment. I could not think of a single one. A fitting irony that the superior, well-bred upper-class Jannie Shean should find the first significant act of her life to be a criminal enterprise controlled by denizens of the deep with few brains, fewer social graces, *but with the desperate courage to challenge fate and defy society*. It was a depressing, humbling thought.

It is, perhaps, a depressing and humbling thought to think that criminals should exercise such discipline to achieve their evil goal, while many of us civilized and sophisticated individuals balk at even the mention of such a harsh word. Discipline may involve sacrifice and possibly pain. No doubt this is why it is much more common to regret having avoided discipline than it is to practice it here and now.

THE DIFFICULTY OF SELF-DISCIPLINE

The matter of resolution and determination in our process of living out and fulfilling the potential of our Golden Shadow reflects the statement which is the third most frequent complaint of people who are approaching the later years of life. As they review the past they note most frequently that they did not take enough risks, second most frequently that they did not assert themselves enough, and thirdly that they lacked self-discipline. For those who make this observation there is the suggestion that this may be the most serious regret of all, for the implication appears to be that if they had exercised more self-discipline, they would have taken more risks and been more assertive.

There is, of course, considerable merit to that speculation; however, it must remain a supposition. Certainly there are many well-disciplined people who still fail to accomplish the goals of the first two complaints. On the other hand, this complaint is important to us for our purposes because resolution and determination are significant factors in our journey toward becoming more and more of what we can be.

In our journey, we are constantly struggling with "what is" and working to transform it into "what can be." This, of course, means change, and change generally meets with stubborn resistance wherever it goes. Our experience is no exception. Therefore, there is sure to be resistance within us to our acting on our insights and discoveries. We have to contend with the momentum of our lives—the negative inertia, if you will. The patterns, habits, attitudes, and characteristics that have inhibited us for many years are not about to be restructured and recombined without resistance. We need, therefore, to be patient with ourselves and not lose courage when it appears that the going is simply too rough.

We continue to love ourselves, rather than be angry or intolerant of our shortcomings as we engage in fulfilling aspects of our potential. We never deny or discount our shortfalls, but we deal consciously with our doubts and our sometimes laggard performance. This is particularly true in our commitment to convert our "I could never do it" into "I will do it." We develop a new mind-set that will empower our resolution and determination. We hold fast to the power of positive expectation even in failure. We always look beyond the immediacy of what presents itself.

It is encouraging to observe that in our larger culture we have become notably able to demonstrate unusual discipline in major areas of our life experience. We have disciplined ourselves to exercise our bodies and abandon sedentary lifestyles. We have disciplined ourselves to follow nutritious eating habits and abandon the improper. We have disciplined ourselves to care for our cardiovascular systems and have given up cigarette smoking.

All this can provide encouragement for the discipline necessary for the undertaking of our journey toward fulfilling the potential of our Golden Shadow. We have demonstrated the ability to discipline ourselves regarding our physical health. No doubt we can act similarly for emotional and spiritual well-being and for equipping and sustaining our journey toward becoming more of what we can be.

THE POWER OF SPIRIT AND WILL

We have spoken consistently or our quest as being a journey. In a very real sense, we have been on a journey through the pages of this book. We began by exploring the situation and predicament of our being. We looked at possibilities—at what we *can* and probably must do. We traced the path of how we can accomplish the task, and we uncovered the possible outcomes of completing it. We considered the possible stumbling blocks to a successful completion, and how we may move beyond them. There now remains the development of the resolution and determination to fulfill the potentials of our Golden Shadow.

We have noted several times that our journey is essentially a spiritual one; therefore, we call upon the transforming power of the Spirit of God within us and pray for strength and support to direct ourselves in the way which we must go. We root and vest our self-discipline in a covenant with ourselves wherein we bind ourselves to pursue diligently what we have *determined* we will do. We pledge our fidelity to this covenant and obligate ourselves to ourselves. Our determination is a definite and firm decision that emotionally and spiritually impels us to fulfill the terms of the covenant and successfully pursue our goal.

We thus blend the power of will and spirit, for our task is greater than a matter of will; it employs belief and faith as well. Belief, faith, and will are inextricably bound. We find the balance between our willingness to receive God's empowerment and our need to exercise the power of our will.

In our self-discipline we draw regularly on the resources of our spiritual dimension. We pray for insight, wisdom, and guidance, and we pray for courage to act on the insight, wisdom, and guidance we receive. We draw on the power of the Spirit of God within us to strengthen our will and support the efforts of our will. We are persuaded, and it is our firm belief, that the will of God for us is that we shall use more and more of the potential we believe we possess because of God's graciousness. We thus empower our will to motivate us to accomplish our task. Again, instead of visualizing ourselves as having to overcome temptations to the contrary, we focus on accomplishing what we set out to do. We remain as positive as we can.

We use meditation as a discipline to direct ourselves. We vividly visualize following the course of action we are directing for ourselves. We use active imagination to visualize images of ourselves succeeding in our tasks. In the midst of discouragement or backsliding on our journey, we accept the experience and envision moving beyond it once again, on our way.

THE DISCIPLINE OF JOURNALING

We use journaling as a discipline to encourage the pursuit of our task. Journaling is not unlike meditation, in that it provides us with a distinct focus on ourselves. Writing in a journal is like writing to ourselves. It is better than talking to ourselves (which may also be quite helpful), because we have the benefit of a written record of the conversation.

Each time we write in our journal we provide ourselves the opportunity to know ourselves a little better. Journaling helps us reflect on matters we may have been consciously ignoring. Because of the noise and interference of normal, everyday activity, some of our psychic material, which is barely "audible" to begin with, is apparent to us only in the quiet of journal writing. We hear ourselves say, "That did not occur to me until I wrote it down and looked at it."

A journal provides a personal, written record. We are often too close to the issues in our lives to develop an appropriate perspective. If we maintain our journal over time, we may look back over it and discover insights that escaped us even at the time of our writing. Furthermore, the written account is helpful in that it provides us with a record of our journey that is undoubtedly more accurate than memory, for memory can often be unreliable. We may not be aware of much progress in living out our discoveries from our Golden Shadow, but our journal account can give us a different perspective from that of memory, and that perspective may happily surprise us.

When we write, we pretend we are talking to a friend, and we write down our conversation. We write, for example, about our concerns, attitudes, feelings, fantasies, reflections on the interpretation of our actions, events, and experiences that elicited feelings, thoughts on what we have read and dramas we have seen, dreams and fantasies, and other people's lives—how they are like or unlike ours. As we write, we focus only on our writing; we do not think about or analyze what we are writing. We do not stop to evaluate or review until we have finished writing.

HELP FROM OTHERS

Other people can help us in the development and ongoing nourishment of our self-discipline. Our traveling companion on our journey inward can be a genuine resource of encouragement. We may also benefit from growth-oriented support groups. Others in the group can help us in our covenant with ourselves and in our commitment to honor it.

I once attended a life-planning workshop with no particular motive in mind, other than perhaps to learn. I discovered in the group, however, that a fear of possible rejection had been encouraging me to drag my feet in completing the manuscript for a book on which I had been working for several years. At the workshop, I covenanted with myself to complete the work by a specific date; for I was enabled to deal with the issue responsible for the delay, and to resolve it. I was able to be faithful to my covenant with myself, and remained grateful to that group experience for its powerful motivation.

Committing to a task can be a major part of accomplishing the task itself. Once we have determined within ourselves that this is what we must do and shall do, we find that the "doing" is not as overwhelming as we had expected. In fact, what we once resisted doing now becomes what we especially want to do; and what once was seen as oppositional may now be seen as supportive.

It is not unusual, in the process of this journey, for us to begin to experience our shadow image in our dreams as actually being helpful to us or rescuing us, whereas before it was something we feared and wanted to get away from. The natural resistance to living out facets of our potential softens as we consistently and faithfully work at it. Our work becomes easier as it becomes more familiar. Accomplishment breeds confidence; we build on each success.

We know that we simply must do this—act on our discoveries, live out and fulfill the potential of our Golden Shadow, and become more and more of what we can be. That is our hope; and, in the last analysis, hope is the alpha and omega of our existence.

Notes

CHAPTER 2. The Journey Inward

20 **In the dream** Carl Jung, *The Archetypes and the Collective Unconscious* (New York: Pantheon Books, 1959), p. 17.
21 **dreamed that he** *Ibid.*, p. 19.
22 **For people who** *Ibid.*, p. 19.
23 **But what shalt** Walter Hilton, *The Scale of Perfection* (London: John M. Watkins, 1948), pp. 126–30.

CHAPTER 4. Overcoming the Interference of the Outer World

40 **to look to** Arthur Koestler, *The Lotus and the Robot* (New York: The Macmillan Company, 1961), p. 276.
48 Herbert Benson and Miriam Klipper, *The Relaxation Response* (New York: William Morrow and Company, Inc., 1975.
William Hulme, *Let the Spirit In* (Nashville: Abingdon, 1979).

CHAPTER 6. Gold in the Mire

73 **envy is a** Marie-Louise von Franz, *An Introduction to the Psychology of Fairy Tales* (Zürich: Spring Publications, 1973), p. 92.

CHAPTER 7. Scoundrels and Saints

80 **the mass murderer . . . years in prison** Viktor Frankl, *Man's Search for Meaning* (New York: Pocket Books-Washington Square Press, 1985), pp. 154–55.

CHAPTER 8. The Undeveloped Self

93 **Man is constantly** Carl Jung, *Psychological Types* (New York: Pantheon Books, 1959), p. 313.
95 **wasting time just** Carl Jung, *Psychology and Religion: West and East* (New York: Pantheon Books, 1958), p. 134.

CHAPTER 9. The Power of Self-Image

112 Nathaniel Branden, *How to Raise Your Self-Esteem* (New York: Bantam, 1987).
William A. Miller, *You Count—You Really Do* (Minneapolis: Augsburg, 1976).

CHAPTER 10. The Willingness to Risk

121 **I am afraid** John Powell, *Why Am I Afraid to Tell You Who I Am?* (Chicago: Argus Communications Co., 1969), p. 12.

CHAPTER 11. The Value of Failure

125 Robert T. Lewis, *Taking Chances: The Psychology of Losing and How to Profit from It* (Boston: Houghton Mifflin Company, 1979), p. 177–78.

CHAPTER 12. The Excitement of Creating

134 **What really happens**   J.R.R. Tolkien, *Tree and Leaf* (New York, Houghton Mifflin Company, 1965), p. 36.

CHAPTER 13. Resolution and Determination

141 **I had another**   Lawrence Sanders, *Caper* (New York: Berkley Publishing Group, 1980), p. 171.